Lead Like
A Father

*What Corporate Leaders
Can Learn from Fathers*

Mark Jeffery

Published by MRK Publishing
Sydney, Australia

ISBN (Paperback): 978-1-7644175-0-1

Cover design: MRK Publishing
Interior design: MRK Publishing
Printed in the country where this book is sold.

Dedication

For my family, who taught me leadership begins at home.

Preface

It wasn't at university where I learnt about leadership, it was when I became a father. I had four children who were uniquely different, and it was up to me to understand how to reach each child independently, nurture what made them unique, rather than try and have the children conform to one style.

I've always been a student of leadership, taking notes, listening and watching. My notes were always meant to be for reflection, refining my own style. The more I kept, and ordered my notes into themes, a started to see something, a simple hypothesis that being a leader at work, is like being a leader at home. What began as personal notes on presence, empathy, and integrity soon found resonance in unexpected places.

I started talking to my mentors, leaders, colleagues and coworkers. I even spoke to friends and sought out publications and recordings of leaders from around the world. All it did was strengthen my view that leading a big organization is a lot like leading a big family. I started hearing leaders say they saw their families in their teams. Fathers said they finally saw their leadership in their parenting.

But this book is not just for parents, and certainly not just for fathers. This is definitely not a book about children. It is a book about people. Fatherhood simply offers a lens, one that sharpens, not restricts, your leadership vision.

You don't need to be a parent for this book to speak to you. While many stories come from fatherhood, the principles throughout these chapters are universal: presence, empathy, discipline, integrity, service, and love. These are human skills long before they are parenting skills, and they matter in every relationship you hold. Simply replace the word "child" with "person you care about" and "family" with "the people who matter most." The lens may come from home, but the lessons apply wherever you lead, influence, or connect with others. Leadership is relational, not parental, and this book is for anyone who wants to lead with more humanity, wisdom, and heart.

This book expands and deepens my own thoughts and approaches to leadership, weaving together timeless wisdom, contemporary research, and the quiet spirituality that underpins both. It's not a manual; it's a mirror.

You'll notice a rhythm throughout this book, stories that begin at home and unfold in leadership, then return home again. Whilst written in the first person, some of the stories and examples from the breakfast table to the boardroom are stories that have been shared with me, from people I trust and respect from over 25 years in leadership.

That rhythm is deliberate. Because leadership, at its best, is not something we perform at work and pause at home. It's something we practice in both places, the same character, the same care, expressed through different languages.

I didn't want it just to be my own thoughts and perspectives so I have brought along the voices that have guided my own personal growth: Daniel Goleman's work on emotional intelligence; Robert Greenleaf's philosophy of servant leadership; Amy Edmondson's research on psychological safety; Stephen Covey's teachings on priorities; Peter Senge's systems thinking; Andy Stanley's faith based leadership, and the reflections of contemporary leaders who remind us that greatness begins with goodness.

As a person that always says "that's great, now what" I have included some Self-Reflective questions and some key takeaways, Habits that Matter, you might like to put into practice.

Whether you lead a household or a hundred people, I hope these pages remind you of one enduring truth: leadership is not about position, it's about posture. It's not about what you achieve, it's about who you are, and how others grow because of you.

So Lead like a Father, with presence, humility, wisdom, and love.

Because the world doesn't need more bosses. It needs more Dads.

The FatherFramed™ Leadership Model

Leadership can feel complicated, a moving sea of frameworks, competencies, expectations, and shifting standards. But when you strip it all back, leadership has always been something far simpler and far deeper: the way we show up for the people who depend on us.

I didn't design the FatherFrame™ by sitting in a boardroom or studying leadership theory. It emerged slowly, quietly, over years of raising children and leading teams, listening to stories, noticing patterns, and capturing the moments that seemed to matter most. I realized that the same qualities that helped my kids feel safe, confident, and supported were the qualities my teams responded to as well.

The more I paid attention, the clearer the pattern became.

When leaders show up with *presence*, people settle.
When leaders hold strong *priorities*, people focus.
When leaders *communicate* with clarity and care, people trust.
When leaders practice *discipline*, people feel secure.
When leaders offer *compassion*, people open up.
When leaders act with *integrity*, people stand taller.
When leaders *serve*, rather than control, people grow.
And when leaders choose to lead with *love*, people flourish.

These weren't just parenting lessons; they were leadership lessons. And they weren't just leadership lessons; they were human lessons.

The FatherFrame™ brings these eight principles together into one simple, coherent philosophy: leadership begins with who you are, not what you do. It is shaped in the quiet, ordinary, often unseen moments where character is formed, and relationships deepen.

And it grows not through grand gestures, but through steady, intentional choices repeated over time.

You don't need to be a parent to embrace the FatherFrame™.

These principles are universal.

They are the way we strengthen others, at home, at work, in friendships, in teams, and in every environment where people look to us for guidance or reassurance.

The FatherFrame™ doesn't replace your leadership style; it grounds it.

It doesn't demand perfection; it encourages practice.

And it doesn't give you a new identity; it helps reveal the one you've been building all along.

As you move through the chapters ahead, you'll see each pillar come to life, not as abstract concepts, but as real human experiences drawn from families, workplaces, and the everyday moments where leadership is quietly shaped. By the end of this book, my hope is that you won't just understand the FatherFrame™, you'll recognize it in yourself.

Because leadership isn't something you perform, it's something you embody. And when you lead with steadiness, clarity, compassion, and love, you create the kind of influence that outlasts roles, titles, or seasons.

This is the FatherFramed™ Leadership Model.
And this is where your journey begins.

Chapter One — Presence: The Quiet Power That Changes Everything

"Presence is the leadership advantage that cannot be faked, when you give someone your full attention, you create safety, trust, and transformation."

Presence is the foundation of all meaningful leadership because it determines whether people feel seen, safe, and valued in your company. In a world overloaded with noise, urgency, and divided attention, the ability to be fully with someone, even for a moment, is now a rare competitive advantage.

Teams and families don't flourish because of lengthy conversations or flawless decisions; they flourish because of consistent, attuned attention. This chapter shows how presence shapes culture, resets emotional tone, and becomes the quiet force that elevates trust, performance, and connection.

FatherFramed™ Leadership begins with Presence, the still, steady center from which all leadership behavior draws its strength. Before we speak, direct, plan, or decide, we lead first with our attention. This chapter explores why presence is more than focus; it is the emotional grounding people feel when you truly show up.

The Space Between Noise

It's 8:42 p.m. and the house is caught in that fragile space between noise and silence, the hum of the refrigerator, the gentle protest of a washing machine mid-cycle, the faint bashing of the electric drums leaking from a closed door. I'm sitting at the kitchen table, surrounded by the remains of the day, empty cups, stray pens, a dog-eared permission note that did not quite make it to a school bag.

My laptop glows like a small moon in the dimness. The email in front of me demands urgency, a late-night decision that could easily wait until morning. But I hover, restless, half-composed sentence flickering in the half-light. Across the room, my young daughter sits cross-legged on the floor, her notebook open, pencil smudges on her hands. The expression on her face is one I know well, that quiet mix of concentration and self-doubt.

"Dad," she says softly, "is this right?"

I do not answer at first. My instinct is to finish the sentence, hit send, tie up the day neatly. But something, almost sacred, makes me look up instead. She is still waiting, hesitant, eyes flicking between me and her page.

And so, I close the laptop. The sound of it feels louder than I expected. A punctuation mark. She looked surprised, then relieved. I cross the room, sit beside her, and together we work through the problem, not just with the arithmetic, but the deeper one: the fear that she might not be enough.

When she gets the answer right, her smile is so unguarded it disarms me. She leans her head briefly against my arm before gathering her papers. "Thanks, Dad." The house feels different, softer and quieter.

Later that night, long after everyone is asleep, I realize what really shifted wasn't her confidence but the atmosphere. The air changed because attention entered it.

Presence is that, a subtle recalibration of the invisible. It doesn't roar or announce itself. It doesn't need applause. It simply *arrives*. And when it does, things around it align.

Presence is the first pillar of what I describe as the FatherFramed™ Leadership Model, because it is the one quality upon which every other leadership behavior rests. If people don't feel you're truly with them, nothing else lands the way it should.

Psychologists John Bowlby and Mary Ainsworth showed that children thrive when they feel securely attached, when they know they can reach and be met with calm, consistent care. The same truth holds for adults in workplaces. Security, not supervision, builds trust

The Modern Poverty of Attention
We often talk about time as our most precious resource, but it isn't. Our most precious resource is Attention.

Time passes whether we use it or not; attention is the decision that gives meaning to time. We're drowning in distractions, dopamine trickles from screens, calendars that mistake activity for significance, conversations where half our minds hover elsewhere.

In the corporate world, presence is now considered a "soft skill." I've always found that ironic. It's the hardest discipline I know. Anyone can send an email; few can give you their eyes without glancing away. Anyone can attend a meeting; few can be *in* the meeting.

When you sit across from a team member who's anxious, or a child who's hurting, and you're fully there, no phone, no agenda, no half-listening, they can feel it. Presence doesn't just register emotionally; it registers biologically. Studies in neuroscience show that our brains literally sync rhythms when we engage deeply with another person, a phenomenon called *interpersonal neural entrainment*. In that resonance, trust grows.

We like to think leadership is built on decisions. But more often, it's built on attention. Presence is the architecture of trust.

The Temperature of a Room
Over the years, I've noticed something curious about leadership: every team, like every family, carries the emotional temperature of its leader. A father's calm steadies a household; a manager's anxiety electrifies an entire office. We teach emotional management to executives in seminars, yet children sense it before they can speak.

I remember a season when one of my teams was under immense strain, budgets shrinking, expectations rising, morale thinning. Every meeting felt like a wrestling match with invisible pressure. One morning, I walked in early, sat at the long timber table, and simply waited. As each person entered, I greeted them quietly, by name, with eye contact, not the perfunctory "morning," but a moment of recognition.

When the meeting began, I didn't start with data. I asked, "Before we talk about numbers, how's everyone really doing?" At first, the question hung awkwardly in the air, this was not what we usually did. Then someone sighed, laughed nervously, and said, "Honestly? Tired." Others nodded. For ten minutes, we just talked, not about deliverables, but about fatigue, motivation, family pressures, and the difficulty of caring too much. By the time we returned to strategy, something invisible had shifted.

14

That day taught me that leadership isn't about tone of voice or charisma; it's about the *energy you permit*. Presence isn't passive, it's *permission-setting*. It tells a room, "You can exhale now. You're safe to be human."

The Discipline of Slowness
In a world that idolizes speed, slowness has become an act of rebellion. But I've learned that slowness isn't laziness, it's accuracy. When we rush, we trade clarity for closure. We respond fast but rarely well.

There's a passage in Viktor Frankl's *Man's Search for Meaning* that changed how I view presence. He writes that between stimulus and response, there is a space, and in that space lies our freedom and growth. That space is presence. It's where reaction transforms into reflection, where instinct meets intention.

Fathers and leaders both live in that space constantly, deciding whether to correct or to listen, to speak or to wait. The wise ones pause. Because every pause is an invitation to wisdom.

In my early managerial years, I didn't pause much. I equated speed with competence. I'd fire off decisions, solve things before understanding them. It took failure to teach me that leadership without reflection is just reaction with better vocabulary.

These days, when someone brings me a problem, I often begin by asking, "What do *you* think?" Sometimes they hesitate, unsure. That's fine. The silence that follows is uncomfortable, but it's sacred. In that silence, ownership begins.

When Presence Feels Inconvenient
Presence sounds noble until it interrupts you. It's easy to talk about mindfulness on a quiet morning; harder when you're exhausted, behind schedule, and someone knocks on your office door with "a quick question."

But the test of presence isn't comfort, it's interruption. Leadership isn't only about setting direction; it's about absorbing disruption without losing composure.

I remember once, years ago, preparing for a presentation that could determine funding for a major initiative. I was in full mental lockdown, rehearsing data points, polishing slides, when a young staff member appeared at my door, visibly shaken. She had made a mistake in a client report that might cost us a partnership. Everything in me wanted to wave her away. But something deeper, call it conscience, call it grace, told me to stop.

We sat down. I listened. She confessed the error, expecting reprimand. Instead, we worked through a recovery plan together. The partnership survived. Months later, she told me that moment was why she stayed with the organization. Not because I had fixed her mistake, but because I had seen *her* in it.

The Presence Paradox

Here's the paradox: the more responsibility you carry, the more presence is demanded of you, yet the less time you feel you have for it. Executives spend their lives multitasking, parents their days managing chaos. We tell ourselves presence will come later, after the meeting, after the quarter, after the kids are older. But later never arrives.

The truth is, presence doesn't require time; it requires attention. Ten minutes of undivided attention can heal more than an hour of distracted company. Presence is qualitative, not quantitative.

It's the same reason a short but heartfelt conversation with a colleague can do more for morale than an elaborate offsite retreat. People remember moments, not meetings.

In family life, I've come to see this too clearly. Children have a kind of radar for divided minds. They can sense when you're nodding but not listening. They don't need your clock; they crave your eyes.

At work, your team is no different. Presence is the only performance review they trust.

Presence as an Act of Service

Robert Greenleaf's idea of servant leadership reframed my understanding of authority. True leadership, he wrote, begins with the desire to serve, to help others grow. Presence is the first service. You can't serve people you don't see.

In one leadership workshop I attended, the facilitator asked the group of managers to recall the best leader they'd ever worked for. Without fail, every story began the same way: "They listened to me." Not "They inspired me." Not "They paid me well." *They listened.*

It's astonishing how rare genuine listening has become in both families and corporations. We hear to reply, not to understand. We listen for weakness, not for truth. Presence flips that script. It says, "You're safe to speak because I'm not waiting for my turn."

Self-Reflection

- When was the last time you felt fully seen, not evaluated or advised, but *seen*?
- What did that experience do to you?
- Now, who in your world needs that same kind of presence from you today?

Habits that Matter

- **Practice the Pause:** Before responding to any question, breathe once and count to three. Let your words emerge from intention, not reflex.

- **Digital Sabbath:** Choose one evening a week to go entirely screen-free for three hours. Notice how your relationships shift.

- **Eye Contact Audit:** In your next meeting or dinner conversation, give your full gaze to each person speaking. Measure how differently you listen.

- **Presence Journal:** Each night, write one moment from the day where you were truly present. Over time, you'll see what matters most.

The Boardroom Mirror

The next morning after that moment with my daughter, I walked into an Exec Meeting that felt eerily like the scene at home the night before, except the anxiety was dressed in suits. The table gleamed, the coffee steamed, and the tension sat like fog. Numbers were slipping, projects behind schedule, and everyone was pretending not to notice.

PowerPoint slides flicked across the wall with clinical precision, charts, ratios, projections. But beneath the data, I sensed something human: fear. People were talking *at* each other, not *with* each other. The CFO interrupted the Marketing Director mid-sentence. The HR head typed furiously, not listening but documenting.

I waited, watching the pace of the conversation accelerate, faster, louder, shallower. When it was my time to speak, I did the most counterintuitive thing I could: I didn't speak. I didn't correct. I didn't rescue. I simply waited.

Eventually, the noise began to collapse under its own weight. People shifted uneasily in their chairs. Silence filled the room. In that stillness, everyone suddenly became aware of their own breathing, and of mine. I leaned forward slightly and said, "Let's take two minutes. No talking. Just breathe."

Someone laughed awkwardly, another rolled their eyes. But they complied. Two minutes of quiet in that room feels like eternity, but it was long enough for the storm to settle.

When we resumed, I said, "What are we really worried about?"

This time, they answered differently, slower, more honestly. "We're tired." "We don't know what's working." "We've stopped trusting our instincts."

That day we didn't fix the spreadsheet, but we fixed the *spirit* of the team. And later, when performance improved, it wasn't because of a better plan; it was because the people finally felt seen again.

Corporate Panic and Emotional Contagion

In organizational psychology, there's a term I often come back to: *emotional contagion*. Daniel Goleman, whose work on emotional intelligence reshaped how we understand leadership, wrote that emotions are as contagious as viruses. The tone of the leader becomes the tone of the room.

If a CEO walks in anxious, the anxiety spreads. If a manager enters defensive, the team mirrors it. But when a leader carries calm, genuine calm, not rehearsed composure, it changes everything.

The most powerful leaders I've worked with aren't the loudest or most visionary; they're the ones who anchor chaos. They don't absorb panic; they metabolize it.

As Daniel Goleman observed in his work on Emotional Intelligence, the most effective leaders are those who manage their own inner state first, because emotion is contagious. The calm leader recalibrates the room before they even speak

Once, during a product crisis at one of the organizations I worked with, a faulty update brought an entire service to a halt. Phones rang off the hook, social media lit up, and the executive team gathered in emergency mode. The air was electric. Everyone was talking at once, voices climbing, adrenaline spiking.

The CEO, a woman in her mid-fifties with decades of quiet resilience, stood still for several seconds, then said softly, "No one moves until we breathe." The room froze. You could almost hear heart rates dropping. Then she said, "We can't think in panic. Let's slow this down."

Within thirty minutes, order returned. Solutions emerged not from authority, but from calm.

Later that day, I asked her how she managed to stay composed. She smiled and said, "I decided years ago that panic is a luxury I can't afford."

That line has stayed with me ever since.

Calm as Strategy

We often frame calmness as personality, something introverts possess or stoics cultivate. But calm is not temperament; it's strategy. It's the discipline of managing your own internal weather before stepping into someone else's storm.

The best leaders don't project serenity because life is easy; they do it because they've learned what chaos costs. They understand that people can't think clearly when they're afraid.

In moments of crisis, everyone looks instinctively toward the leader, not for information, but for orientation. They're asking, *Are we safe? Are you steady?*

Presence answers before words do.

There's a physics to it, your emotional energy becomes the template others calibrate to. The psychologist Sigal Barsade described this as "affective synchrony." Teams unconsciously align with the leader's emotional rhythm, whether that rhythm is anxiety or assurance.

I once had a team member come into my office and say "You know why I'm calm, because you're calm" just as we were about to undertake an unannounced standards audit.

So, if your presence says "We're okay," the team doesn't just hear it, they feel it. And that physiological shift is what allows creativity, focus, and collaboration to return.

This applies just as much at home. A child's nervous system mirrors a parent's before they ever understand language. When you walk into a room, your presence preaches a sermon your words can't.

Stillness in the Storm
Presence doesn't always mean stillness on the outside. Sometimes it's active, the quiet within motion.

I once worked with a manager who was known for her "still eye in the storm." When deadlines loomed and tempers rose, she would methodically clear her desk, pour a cup of tea, and ask, "What's the most human thing we can do right now?" That question became her compass.

I watched her defuse conflicts, reframe failures, and comfort teams not by avoiding emotion, but by holding space for it. Her calm was not absence of feeling, it was mastery of meaning.

When people trust your calm, they give you their truth.

And that's when leadership becomes transformation, not transaction.

Lessons from Satya Nadella
When Satya Nadella took over as CEO of Microsoft in 2014, the company was brilliant but brittle, full of talent but suffocating under competition and internal politics. Nadella didn't begin by changing the strategy; he changed the *tone*.

He went on a listening tour. He spent months meeting engineers, designers, and frontline staff, not to talk, but to ask. His mantra became "empathy makes you a better innovator."

He modelled a leadership presence that listened before it spoke. And it worked. Within five years, Microsoft's culture shifted from defensive to collaborative. Its market value soared. But more importantly, its people rediscovered pride in belonging.

What Nadella proved was this: presence isn't soft power. It's sustainable power.

The modern leader's edge is no longer information, it's *integration*. The ability to be fully present with people, data, and purpose all at once.

The Weight of Invisible Work
Presence in leadership is costly because it requires what I call *emotional overhead*, the unseen work of staying steady for others. It's the weight of caring without collapsing.

Every father knows this feeling, the quiet burden of being the calm one when everyone else unravels. Every executive knows it too, that strange loneliness of holding a team's anxiety while hiding your own.

Presence demands emotional endurance. And endurance requires renewal.

One of the most overlooked skills of great leaders is how they recharge. They guard solitude as fiercely as meetings. They treat reflection as fuel, not indulgence. They know that attention, like any resource, depletes if not restored.

Personally, I've learned to protect one small ritual: before major meetings, I sit alone for three minutes, phone off, eyes closed. I imagine the people I'm about to lead, their stresses, their hopes, their humanity, and I silently pray for calm. Then I walk in.

That prayer, or meditation, or mindful breath, whatever you should call it, it's a strategy. It's how we bring peace into places that don't have it.

When Presence Requires Courage

Not all presence feels serene. Sometimes it feels confrontational, the courage to stay in a hard conversation rather than escape it.

In one particularly turbulent management season, two department heads were in open conflict. Everyone else avoided them, including me, at first. But the tension was poisoning the culture.

So one afternoon, I invited them both into my office. "We're not leaving until we understand each other," I said.

For an hour, they argued. Voices rose. Accusations flew. I didn't intervene; I stayed. My only rule was respect. When they paused, I asked questions, not to mediate, but to surface meaning. Gradually, emotion gave way to empathy. One said, "I thought you didn't value my work." The other said, "I thought you were trying to replace me." Both were wrong, but both felt real.

By the end of the meeting, they weren't friends, but they were allies again.

That's the thing about presence: it's not about peacekeeping. It's about *truth-keeping*. Sometimes the most loving thing you can do as a leader is to hold tension long enough for truth to emerge.

Self-Reflection

- When you walk into your workplace, what tone follows you?

- Do you enter rooms ready to contribute or to control?

- How does your internal state, unspoken, unseen, shape the people you lead?

Habits that Matter

- **Two-Minute Rule:** Before any major meeting, take two minutes of silence. Let your heart rate settle. Don't enter chaos carrying chaos.

- **The Emotional Audit:** At the end of each week, write down moments when your tone influenced others, for better or worse. What patterns emerge?

- **The Empathy Loop:** In your next one-on-one, summarize what you heard before you respond. Watch how safety changes honesty.

- **The Reset Ritual:** When frustration builds, step outside, find a horizon, a literal horizon, and look far. The distance restores perspective.

The Inner Work of Stillness

Stillness is one of the most misunderstood words in leadership. People imagine it as retreat, a kind of withdrawal from responsibility, an escape from the noise. But I've come to see it differently.

Stillness isn't the absence of motion; it's the anchoring of it. It's the ability to hold your internal center while the world around you moves.

For me, the journey toward stillness didn't begin in a meditation class or a leadership seminar. It began in a car.

The Carpark Lesson

It was years ago, on a morning already running late. I had just dropped my children off at school after a chaotic breakfast, spilled milk, lost shoes, small arguments that had no winners. My mind was already racing ahead to the day's agenda: a presentation to the CEO, a performance review, a thousand emails waiting for response.

I parked outside the office, turned off the engine, and for the first time in a long time, did nothing.
No music, no phone, no radio. Just the hum of silence around me.

For a moment, the stillness felt uncomfortable, like an uninvited guest. My thoughts, unfiltered and loud, rose to the surface: *You're behind. You're unprepared. You're not enough.*

And then, gradually, something softened. I breathed deeply and realized that this, this quiet, awkward, necessary pause, was the missing ingredient in my leadership.

I had mastered productivity, but not presence. I could run meetings, deliver strategies, and juggle ten priorities, but I could not sit still.

That was the morning I learned a truth that would change my rhythm forever:

Leadership begins before the first meeting. It begins in the car, in the silence, in the space between breath and responsibility.

That small act of stillness has since become my ritual. Three minutes every morning before walking into work. Three minutes to become aware of the weight I carry and the energy I'll release. Three minutes to decide who I'll be before I decide what I'll do.

The Battle for Inner Space
Most leaders I've met are not short on intelligence; they're short on space. Their days are overfilled, their calendars double-booked, their minds never silent.
But leadership, like fatherhood, depends on emotional bandwidth, the capacity to think, feel, and discern without being drowned by noise.

The challenge isn't that we don't have time; it's that we don't protect it.

We fill every margin with consumption, another podcast, another meeting, another scroll through headlines. But reflection requires *margin*. Wisdom needs white space.

Peter Senge, in *The Fifth Discipline*, wrote about systems thinking, how everything is interconnected, and how actions echo in unseen ways. Stillness is how we start seeing those echoes. When you slow down enough to notice patterns, you realize most crises are not random; they're rhythmic. They repeat because we react the same way each time.

Stillness helps you recognize the loops, in your team, in your family, in yourself, and choose differently.

Self-Regulation: The Hidden Leadership Skill

Daniel Goleman's framework for emotional intelligence includes self-awareness and self-regulation. These sound academic, but they're deeply human. Self-regulation is simply this: the ability to notice what you feel without letting it own you.

In my twenties, I mistook composure for control. I'd enter meetings trying to *look* calm while my mind ran a hundred miles an hour. I'd keep my tone even, my words measured, but my impatience always leaked through. People can sense false calm like a tremor beneath the surface.

Now, when I feel frustration rising, I pause, not to suppress it, but to understand it. What is this emotion trying to tell me? Is it about them, or is it about me? That question alone has saved relationships, teams, and opportunities.

Real stillness doesn't mean you feel less. It means you feel *fully*, and respond wisely.

The Private Room of the Soul

There's a line from the mystic Thomas Merton that I often return to:

"There is in all visible things an invisible fecundity, a dimmed light, a hidden wholeness."

Stillness is how you touch that hidden wholeness.
It's the quiet conversation between you and your conscience, a dialogue that no boardroom can host, no spreadsheet can quantify.

Fathers know this space. It's where you sit late at night, wondering if you handled something well. It's where you pray, or simply breathe, asking for patience you don't yet have. It's where you remind yourself that love is not weakness, that gentleness is still strength.

Leaders need that same inner room. Without it, we become mechanical, efficient but hollow. Stillness fills the soul's tank so that kindness, clarity, and courage can flow again.

How Stillness Reframes Leadership
Stillness changes not just how we lead, but how we perceive the world. It turns noise into information, urgency into discernment.

I once witnessed a manager who was brilliant but reactive. Every problem felt like a personal failure, every complaint an attack. He was perpetually tired, not from overwork, but from overreacting.

I recommended he start each morning by writing one question at the top of his notebook:

"What does this moment require from me, not what do I feel, not what do I fear, but what is needed?"

That single practice changed him. He stopped fighting fires and started building firebreaks. He learned to listen without defending, to act without proving. His team flourished.

Stillness gives you that gift, the pause between impulse and wisdom. It allows you to *respond* instead of *react*.

Humility: The Companion of Stillness
If stillness is the posture of awareness, humility is the posture of openness.

The two are inseparable. You can't be still if you need to prove yourself; and you can't be humble if you're afraid of silence.

In both family life and leadership, humility isn't thinking less of yourself, it's thinking of yourself less. It's making room for others to be right, for truth to arrive from somewhere else.

I learned this lesson one afternoon while leading a difficult negotiation between two departments. Tensions were high, egos higher. Each side was certain of its righteousness.

I had prepared meticulously, convinced I could mediate the outcome. But halfway through the meeting, it became clear that my presence was making things worse, both sides were performing for my approval.

So I stopped talking. I closed my notebook and said, "I think I'm part of the noise right now. Let's take a break. You two keep talking, without me."

They looked stunned. I left the room, walked outside, and waited. Twenty minutes later, they emerged, calmer, smiling slightly. They had found the compromise themselves.

Stillness sometimes means *stepping back* so that others can step up.
That's humility in action, trusting that the solution doesn't need your signature to have your spirit.

The Practice of Silence
Silence has become rare in both homes and offices. We fear it, fill it, run from it. But silence is not emptiness; it's ecosystem.

When I facilitate workshops, I often begin with sixty seconds of silence. It's remarkable to watch, the awkward fidgeting, the nervous laughter, the shuffling of papers. But within those sixty seconds, something sacred happens: the room synchronizes. Minds settle. Presence rises.

Afterwards, participants often say, "That was strange... but grounding."

That's the point.

Silence resets our nervous systems. It reminds us that wisdom doesn't shout; it whispers.

When I'm home, I try to weave silence into the noise of family life, the unspoken ritual of watching the sunrise with coffee, of driving together without music, of letting conversation emerge naturally instead of forcing it. Those moments build invisible bridges.

Stillness, practiced in silence, doesn't disconnect us from others; it connects us *more deeply*.

When Stillness Feels Impossible
Some seasons make stillness hard, loss, crisis, burnout. When the phone won't stop ringing and decisions carry real consequences, the idea of "finding peace" feels almost insulting.

In those moments, I remember something a former leader once told me:

"When you can't find peace, practice presence. Peace will follow."

Stillness doesn't require serenity; it requires surrender. Sometimes, the bravest thing you can do is simply to *stop running inside yourself*.

During the pandemic, when uncertainty and fear dominated every conversation, I made a habit of walking the same short path each morning. Not for exercise, for grounding. Each tree, each sound of birds, each patch of sunlight became a quiet reminder that steadiness was still possible.

The world was loud, but within that small radius of stillness, I could hear my own soul again.

Self-Reflection

- When was the last time you sat in silence long enough to hear your own thoughts settle?

- What fears or insecurities tend to rise when you slow down, and what might they be teaching you?

- How could stillness before a decision change the outcome, not by adding information, but by restoring perspective?

Habits that Matter

- **Three-Minute Margin:** Before major meetings, or before walking through the door at home, take three minutes of silence. No phone, no planning, just breathing.

- **Write to Listen:** When your mind feels noisy, write your thoughts unfiltered for five minutes. Seeing them on paper brings clarity to chaos.

- **Daily Reset:** Choose one activity (like making coffee or walking the dog) to do in total silence each day. Let it become your anchor.

- **The Humility Check:** In your next conflict, ask: "What might I be wrong about?" Write down the answer privately, not to expose weakness, but to protect wisdom

The Ripple Effect

Culture doesn't begin with slogans or strategies, it begins with how a leader walks into a room. Every tone of voice, every pause, every look becomes a signal that ripples through the system. Presence and stillness, when practiced consistently, create what I call *emotional gravity*, an invisible pull toward steadiness. People begin to orbit that calm. They align themselves around it, often without knowing why.

When I first began to lead large teams, I assumed culture came from what I said, the vision I cast, the policies I wrote, the enthusiasm I projected. Over time, I learned that culture actually grows from what I repeat. What I celebrate, what I tolerate, what I pause for, those things become the atmosphere.

And presence is the purest signal in that atmosphere. When leaders are grounded, the people they lead begin to breathe differently.

How Stillness Scales

We often talk about scaling systems or operations, but rarely about scaling emotional health.
Yet, emotional health is what keeps an organization, or a family, from fracturing under pressure.

I once took over a department known for its speed and efficiency but plagued by burnout. People were polite but detached, meetings efficient but lifeless. Targets were met, but joy had gone missing. I could have introduced a wellness program, a motivational speaker, a staff survey. Instead, I began each Monday morning meeting with something radical: silence.

For sixty seconds, no one spoke. We just sat, phones away, laptops closed, eyes unfocused, and breathed. At first, it was awkward. You could feel the discomfort rise. But gradually, something changed. People began to arrive earlier, settle faster, speak slower. The energy in the room softened.

After several weeks, one of my team members said, "I don't know why, but I feel like we work better now."

Stillness, it turns out, scales faster than strategy. When you model it, others catch it.

In leadership literature, this is often called *emotional contagion* or *mirroring*, but I prefer a simpler term: resonance. Humans are tuning forks, we attune to each other's emotional frequencies. Presence creates resonance.

And resonance is the foundation of trust.

The Family Table Experiment
At home, I tried a similar experiment.

For years, our dinner table had become a logistical hub, a place of instructions, reminders, corrections. "Don't forget your homework." "Who's on dishes tonight?" "Stop scrolling."

One evening, I declared a new rule: no phones, no corrections, no agendas, just conversation. At first, it felt unnatural. The kids looked suspicious. My wife smiled politely, knowing I was up to something.

I started with a simple question: "What was the best part of your day?"

It was clumsy at first, one-word answers, long pauses, a few sarcastic jokes. But over the next few weeks, something miraculous unfolded. The table started to come alive again. Stories replaced silence. Laughter returned. The room began to feel like a place of refuge, not instruction.

It reminded me of something Peter Drucker once said:

"Culture eats strategy for breakfast."

At home or at work, you can't legislate warmth. You can only model it.

Stillness becomes contagious when it's felt, not enforced.

The Meeting That Changed Everything

Several years ago, I was a part of an executive team caught in what they described as "decision paralysis." We had smart people, good data, and shared values, but endless debate. Everyone spoke, few listened.

On the first day, I sat through two hours of discussion without saying a word. I watched as ideas ricocheted like tennis balls, constant volleys, no rallies. At one point, our CEO stopped them and asked, "What are you hearing right now, not what's being said, but what's *underneath* it?"

Silence. Then someone said, "I think we're all just trying to prove we belong."

It was the most honest thing spoken all day. That moment broke something open. People began to listen again, not to win, but to understand.

By the end of the session, one of the executives said, "I think we just had our first real conversation in months."

Presence doesn't fix dysfunction; it reveals it. And once revealed, dysfunction begins to heal.

That's why leaders who cultivate stillness often end up leading healthier cultures, not because they have all the answers, but because they create space for truth to surface.

The Emotional Echo

The psychologist and leadership researcher Annie McKee once wrote that leaders are "emotional transmitters." Whether they intend to or not, they broadcast emotional signals that echo throughout their organizations.

I've seen this in the smallest gestures. A CEO who sighs in frustration during a meeting doesn't realize that the sigh will be repeated, amplified, in the hallways hours later. A parent who glances at their phone during a story sends the unspoken message: *You're less interesting than this notification.*

Our presence teaches others how much they matter.

The ripple effect of attention is real, measurable even. Gallup's research on engagement consistently shows that employees who feel their managers notice and value them are far more productive, loyal, and innovative.

And at home, children who grow up feeling consistently seen develop stronger self-regulation and empathy. They learn emotional literacy not through lectures but through the mirror of presence.

If leadership is influence, then presence is the language it speaks.

Stories that Multiply

When I worked in aged care, I learned more about leadership from residents than from textbooks.

One man, a retired teacher in his nineties, used to sit by the window every morning, greeting each staff member by name. I once asked him why he did it. He smiled and said, "Because if I start the day with kindness, everyone else starts softer too."

He was right. Within weeks, his small ritual had changed the mood of the whole wing. Staff began smiling more, speaking slower. The ripple spread.

He wasn't a manager or a strategist, he was a man practicing presence.

And he led an entire microculture without ever trying to.

That experience taught me something vital: authority is borrowed, but influence is earned.

And influence, at its purest, comes from how we make people *feel safe enough to be human.*

Presence and Performance
Too often, leaders separate performance from culture, as if results can be engineered in isolation. But culture is the soil in which performance grows.

When a leader practices presence, psychological safety increases, and that, as Amy Edmondson's research shows, is the single greatest predictor of team learning and innovation.

Teams that feel safe don't waste energy hiding mistakes or managing impressions. They use that energy to create. They take risks. They recover faster.

In one organization where I was a leader, we replaced performance reviews with what we called *Development Meetings.* Instead of ranking people, we asked three questions:

1. What did you learn this quarter?

2. Where did you grow?

3. What would you try if fear wasn't a factor?

Within six months, the innovation metrics rose, not because we demanded creativity, but because we stopped punishing imperfection. Presence had become institutionalized.

Stillness at the top became courage at the bottom.

The Cost of Disconnection
There's a quiet tragedy I see in many modern workplaces, leaders who are admired but not known. They've built reputations, not relationships.

I've sat in offices where subordinates spoke of their bosses with both awe and distance: "They're brilliant... but unapproachable." It's as if competence came at the cost of connection.

Presence closes that distance. When a leader looks someone in the eye, asks how they are, and actually listens to the answer, something sacred happens: hierarchy collapses, humanity reappears.

In homes, it's no different. I've watched fathers who command respect but rarely earn affection. They wonder why their children obey but don't confide. The reason is simple, presence has been replaced by performance.

Love, in leadership or parenting, is measured not by how much you do, but by how much of yourself you give.

From Ripple to Tide
When presence becomes embedded in culture, the ripple becomes a tide. It moves quietly but powerfully through the organization.

I once attended a retreat for mid-level managers. On the final day, one participant stood up and said, "You know, I came here expecting strategies. But I think the real strategy is peace."

Everyone nodded. They had discovered what I believe to be one of the great paradoxes of leadership:

Stillness is not the opposite of progress; it's the engine of it.

When calm becomes culture, creativity flows. When attention becomes habit, innovation rises. When empathy becomes the default, people stay, not because they have to, but because they want to.

And when that happens, leadership ceases to be about control. It becomes about cultivation.

Self-Reflection

- What atmosphere follows you, one of tension or one of trust?

- If someone described your leadership presence in one word, what would it be?

- Where in your culture, family or organization, has hurry replaced humanity?

Habits that Matter

- **Model the Pause:** Begin every team meeting with sixty seconds of silence or gratitude. Let calm become a shared habit.

- **Story Circles:** Once a month, invite team members to share one story of kindness, resilience, or learning. Connection grows through narrative.

- **Presence Audit:** Ask three trusted people, at home or work, "How do you feel when I walk into a room?" Listen without defense.

- **Anchor Rituals:** Create one daily practice that grounds your team, a morning check-in, a shared reflection, a walk-and-talk instead of an email.

The Rhythm of Presence

If the earlier parts of this chapter explored presence as a feeling, a practice, and a force of culture, this section gathers those lessons and places them in your hands, as a Rhythm. These are not rules or strategies; but stances. They are the quiet, repeatable actions that turn theory into transformation.

When I think of the rhythm, I don't imagine corporate frameworks or presentation diagrams, I imagine a father in a kitchen late at night, sitting with his thoughts, replaying the day and whispering to himself: *Tomorrow, I'll try again.*

That's what this section is, the simple wisdom of trying again, with more attention and a gentler heart.

Presence as Strategic Stillness

Stillness isn't absence. It's precision.

It's the moment before the sentence, the breath before the response, the pause before the decision that changes everything.

In leadership, stillness buys you clarity; in fatherhood, it buys you grace.

When a child lashes out or a colleague makes a mistake, the temptation is always to fix or correct. But presence teaches us that fixing is often the enemy of understanding.

I've learned to ask one quiet question before responding to any emotional situation, whether at home or in the boardroom:

"What does this moment need from me, not what do I *want* to give it?"

That question slows me down long enough to lead with purpose instead of pride.

Presence doesn't eliminate mistakes; it multiplies meaning. When you stay still long enough, others discover their own capacity for wisdom. That's how trust begins, not from direction, but from permission.

A father doesn't need to control the atmosphere to shape it; he needs only to be still enough for others to find balance around him.

Calm is Contagious
If emotions spread, then calm is leadership's greatest contagion.

You can enter a meeting in turmoil or a home in chaos, and within moments, everyone will begin to mirror the emotional weather you bring.

The most seasoned leaders I've met understand this intuitively. One CEO told me, "My first job is to set the temperature." Another father put it differently: "If I lose my cool, my kids lose their compass."

The neuroscience backs them both.

Our limbic systems, the brain's emotional core, are wired to synchronize with those around us. It's why you feel anxious near someone tense, and soothed near someone peaceful.
The leader's nervous system becomes the organization's thermostat.

Richard Boyatzis' research on resonant leadership calls this emotional attunement, when a leader's calm presence activates positive resonance across a team.

The challenge, of course, is that calm doesn't come naturally in chaos. It must be *trained*. It's a discipline of breath, of prayer, of reflection, of pausing before sending the email that feels good but does harm.

Over the years, I've created a small ritual for crisis moments, one I call the *10-Second Sabbath.*
When adrenaline rises, I stop, take a slow breath, and silently say: *This moment doesn't need my panic; it needs my presence.*

It's astonishing how much better decisions become when panic is absent from the equation.

Listening as Leadership
In most corporate settings, the word "leadership" conjures images of speech, the visionary talk, the persuasive meeting, the bold declaration.

But the most transformative moments I've ever witnessed as a leader came not from talking, but from listening.

There's a scene I'll never forget: a team member sitting across from me, tears welling as she confessed that she felt invisible. "You're always kind," she said, "but you're not *here.*"
It was one of the most painful compliments I've ever received.

I had mistaken being *nice* for being *present.*
But niceness doesn't heal; attention does.

Listening is the purest form of love in leadership. It says, *You don't need to earn my attention, you already have it.*

Fathers know this instinctively. A child rarely asks for advice; they ask to be seen. When we listen without fixing, they grow stronger. When we rush to rescue, they stay dependent.

The same applies to teams. Listening turns followers into thinkers.

True presence listens not to solve, but to understand. And once people feel understood, they will give you their best work, their honest truth, and their enduring loyalty.

Grace Sustains Growth
You will fail at presence. Constantly.

You'll check your phone during dinner. You'll cut someone off mid-story. You'll lose patience when grace was the better option.

But failure is not the end of presence; it's the proof that you need it.

Grace, the willingness to begin again without shame, is what keeps presence alive.

I used to think leadership credibility depended on perfection. I believed that authority meant never showing weakness.
But the longer I lead, the more I realize that humility doesn't diminish authority; it *defines* it.

The moments when I've returned to apologize, to a colleague, a child, or a friend, have built more trust than all my polished speeches combined.

People don't need flawless leaders; they need human ones.

Presence doesn't mean never failing. It means always returning.

Presence and Purpose
Without purpose, presence collapses into passivity.

You can be kind, calm, and attentive, and still lead nowhere. Purpose is what gives presence its compass.

Purpose answers the question: *Why am I here?*

In a family, the answer might be *to raise people of character, not comfort.*

In a business, it might be *to create value that uplifts, not just profits.*

Purpose turns stillness into strength. It ensures that calm doesn't become complacency, and compassion doesn't become compromise.

When presence and purpose align, leadership becomes magnetic, people follow not because they must, but because they trust.

And here's the deeper truth: purpose is always relational. It's never about ego or achievement; it's about service. The purpose of leadership is to make others better. The purpose of fatherhood is the same.

The Legacy of Attention
Someday, long after we're gone, the people we've led, in homes or in organizations, won't remember our quarterly results or our management styles. They'll remember how it *felt* to be around us.

They'll remember whether our eyes met theirs, whether our tone softened or sharpened, whether our presence steadied or scattered.

One day, your child might describe you to their own children and say, "He was always there." One day, a former employee might tell a new leader, "She really listened."

That's legacy, not the achievements you leave behind, but the atmosphere you leave behind.

Presence is the invisible architecture of legacy. Every moment of attention becomes a brick in that unseen structure. And someday, when others find refuge in the calm you once carried, you'll know it was worth every pause.

Self-Reflections

1. Who in your life embodies calm, that quiet confidence that steadies a room? What can you learn from how they move, not just what they say?

2. When do you most often retreat from presence, under stress, distraction, fear? What might it look like to remain open instead of reactive?

3. What legacy of attention are you building? When people speak of you, will they recall your achievements or your atmosphere?

Habits that Matter

- **The Presence Pledge:** Each morning, choose one person, at work or home, to give your full attention to for ten uninterrupted minutes. No devices, no multitasking.

- **Ritual of Return:** When you notice you've drifted into distraction, simply name it ("I'm not here") and return without guilt. Awareness redeems the moment.

- **The Calm Audit:** At the end of each week, note one moment when your calm influenced others and one when your anxiety did. Learn from both.

- **Legacy Letters:** Write a short note to someone you lead or love, describing a quality in them you've noticed recently. Presence becomes permanent when expressed.

Closing Thought

Presence is love expressed through attention. It's the slow heartbeat beneath every healthy family, every flourishing company, every meaningful life.

It's not a style or a skill; it's a way of being, a quiet declaration that *you matter enough for me to be here, now.*

Presence is the first anchor of the FatherFrame™, the still point from which all meaningful leadership begins.

The world is full of noise, performance, and posturing. But the leaders and fathers who change lives are those who choose to stay still long enough to listen.

"The greatest illusion of leadership, is that presence is optional."

The greatest truth is that it never was.

Presence tunes our attention to what matters; priorities determine what we do with that attention. Once you learn to slow down enough to truly see yourself, your people, your pressures, the next challenge becomes choosing wisely.

Every leader, like every parent, eventually faces the same tension: you cannot hold everything. Something must be released so something better can rise. And so the next chapter invites you into the courageous discipline of doing less, better, of shaping your life and leadership around what matters most.

Chapter Two — Priorities: Doing Less, Better

"Great leaders aren't defined by how much they do, but by the courage to choose what matters and the discipline to release what doesn't."

Leaders are overwhelmed not because they have too little time, but because they are carrying too many competing commitments. This chapter reframes productivity by cutting through the illusion that doing more creates more impact.

Instead, it explores the discipline of discerning what truly matters, and the courage to let go of the rest. Whether in a busy household or a fast-moving organization, clarity of priority enables clarity of mind, decision-making, and wellbeing. When leaders choose less, they gain focus, energy, and integrity, and the people around them do too.

Priorities form the second pillar of the FatherFrame™ because clarity is the antidote to the overwhelm that weakens leaders and cultures alike. When we choose what matters most, we create order not just in our own lives but in the environments we lead. This chapter explores the courage and discipline required to do less, better.

The Illusion of Everything

It was one of those mornings that felt like a sprint before it even began. The kind where you open your inbox and realize it's already won the day before you've had a chance to fight back.

I'd barely taken the first sip of coffee when a colleague appeared at my door with that unmistakable expression that says, "This will only take a minute," which, of course, it never does.

By 9:00 a.m., my schedule was already fractured, overlapping meetings, decisions delayed, requests piling like leaves in a storm.

Every part of the organization wanted something: reports, strategy updates, signatures, answers. Every part of me wanted to disappear.

At home, things weren't much different. The family calendar was an ecosystem of motion, school events, sports, orthodontic appointments, birthdays, reminders. Life had become a blur of obligations stitched together by good intentions and exhaustion.

That evening, sitting in the car after another forever-hour day, I asked myself a question that felt both simple and devastating:

"How did I become so busy doing things that don't matter?"

Parenting researcher Justin Coulson often says the greatest gift we can give our children is 'less of our schedule and more of our presence.' The same is true in leadership. Busyness can look like productivity, but it's often avoidance dressed as virtue.

The Addiction to More

There's a strange irony in modern leadership. The very people tasked with creating focus are often the most distracted. The more successful you become, the more fragmented your attention grows. The inbox swells, the calendar compresses, and suddenly, you're managing *volume* instead of *vision*.

Busyness becomes identity.

We wear exhaustion like a badge, as if depletion proves devotion.

In one leadership retreat I attended, the group of executives was asked to describe their biggest challenge in a single word. Half of them wrote "focus." The rest wrote "time." But as we unpacked their responses, it became clear they were really describing *the same problem*. They didn't have time because they didn't have focus, and they didn't have focus because they were trying to do everything.

Modern culture celebrates the omnipresent leader, the multitasker, the hustler, the achiever. But beneath that applause hides a quiet truth: doing more rarely makes you better; it just makes you *busier*.

Greg McKeown's *Essentialism* calls this the "undisciplined pursuit of more." I've seen it destroy clarity, creativity, and health. I've also seen it in myself, in the way I'd fill silence with tasks, measure worth in emails sent, and mistake movement for momentum.

I once heard someone describe leadership as "the art of intentional neglect." The phrase unsettled me until I realized it's the secret most effective leaders share. They know that saying yes to everything is the fastest path to mediocrity.

The Father's Mirror
The realization hit me hardest not in an office, but at a family barbecue.

I'd spent most of the day answering work calls in between half-finished conversations. My young son, eight at the time, tugged at my sleeve and said, "Dad, you're always on your phone."

His words landed like a verdict.

That night, I lay awake thinking about the example I was setting. What was I teaching him, that presence is optional, that attention is negotiable, that life is something you manage, not live?

I began to see the parallel between my home and my office. My kids, like my team, weren't asking for more of me; they were asking for *the real me*. They didn't need a father who was everywhere, they needed one who was *anywhere fully*.

The same is true of leadership. Your people don't need constant access; they need meaningful availability. The myth of omnipresence dilutes effectiveness. True leadership is not about being everywhere, it's about being where it counts.

The Weight of False Urgency
One of the most insidious aspects of modern work is the illusion of urgency.

Everything feels critical because everything is connected. Notifications create false alarms, emails masquerade as emergencies, and our minds, addicted to dopamine and validation, can't tell the difference.

There's an old Navy SEAL mantra that says, "Slow is smooth, and smooth is fast."

The best soldiers, surgeons, and leaders understand that frantic motion is the enemy of precision.

In one of my earlier roles, I led a team that prided itself on responsiveness. We answered every email, solved every issue, attended every meeting. We were admired, and exhausted. When we finally paused to review performance metrics, the data was sobering: we were working harder than ever but achieving less impact.

So, we made a radical choice, we began to *ignore things*.
We stopped responding to non-essential emails. We consolidated meetings. We eliminated projects that weren't directly tied to outcomes.

Within months, everything improved, not because we did more, but because we did less with intention.

That's when I learned: urgency is often just a symptom of unclear priorities.

Leadership and the Cost of Clutter
Clutter in leadership isn't physical; it's cognitive. It's the noise of indecision, the weight of unfinished thoughts, the constant pivot from one half-focus to another.

A Harvard study on decision fatigue found that the average executive makes over 200 small decisions a day, most of them irrelevant. The cost? Reduced creativity, increased stress, and poor judgment by day's end.

Presence and prioritization are intimately linked. You cannot be fully present when your mind is divided across too many directions.

That's why I've come to see focus as a moral discipline. It's not just about efficiency; it's about honoring the people who depend on your clarity.

When I say no to distractions, I'm not just protecting my productivity; I'm protecting their trust.

Reframing Success

There's a moment in every leader's life when ambition collides with wisdom. It's when you realize that success isn't about adding more, but about refining what already exists.

I've sat in rooms with brilliant executives who could double revenue but couldn't name what truly gave them joy. I've watched parents who provided everything their children could want but struggled to give them the one thing they needed most, *attention without agenda.*

The truth is, doing everything is easy. Doing the right thing is hard.

The first step toward doing less, better, is to redefine what success means. For me, it's no longer about scale or applause. It's about alignment, between values, actions, and relationships.

When those align, peace follows. And peace, I've found, is the surest indicator of real progress.

Self-Reflection

1. Where in your life are you confusing motion with meaning?

2. Which commitments drain energy but add no real value, to your work or to your family?

3. What might change if your definition of success included peace as a metric?

Habits that Matter

- **Audit the Noise:** For one week, keep a "distraction log." Every time you switch tasks or respond impulsively, note it. Review where your focus leaks.

- **Schedule Stillness:** Block 15 minutes daily for thinking, not doing. Protect it as fiercely as a meeting.

- **The Family Parallel:** Choose one family ritual each week, dinner, drive, walk, and make it device-free. Notice what deepens.

- **Ask the Filter Question:** Before saying yes, ask: *Does this align with what matters most right now?*

The Discipline of Discerning

The word *discernment* has fallen out of fashion in the age of analytics.

We talk about metrics, insights, and data, but not discernment. Yet it's the quiet force that separates movement from meaning, noise from necessity, and leadership from mere management.

Discernment is the ability to see clearly when the world rewards confusion. It's the skill of knowing not just what's right, but *what's right for now.*

The best leaders I've known don't make faster decisions, they make *fewer, better* ones. They have learned to listen for patterns beneath pressure, to sense when to act and when to wait.
And that capacity, to perceive, to pause, to prioritize, is what I call the discipline of discerning.

The Weight of Too Many Good Things

When I first became a General Manager, I was intoxicated by possibility. Everything felt urgent, everything promising. My office wall was lined with project timelines and ideas scribbled on whiteboards. Every new initiative looked like opportunity, and I wanted them all.

But "too many good things" is one of leadership's most deceptive dangers.

By the end of that first year, our team was exhausted. We had progress reports for everything and momentum for nothing. One day, a colleague walked into my office and said, "Mark, we're drowning in great ideas."

That phrase stopped me cold. *Drowning in great ideas.*

In that moment, I realized that not every good thing is a necessary thing. Leadership isn't about choosing between right and wrong, it's about choosing between *right and almost right*.

Discernment is the art of subtraction, of removing the unnecessary so the essential can breathe.

The 3 A.M. Test

I have a friend who has a rule he calls the *3 A.M. test.* It's simple: If a decision still feels right at 3 A.M., when your ego is asleep and your conscience is awake, it's probably the right one.

I learned this the hard way.

Years ago, I approved a partnership deal that looked perfect on paper, financially strong, strategically aligned, publicly appealing. But something inside me hesitated. Not a red flag exactly, more like static.
I ignored it.

Six months later, the partnership collapsed under values misalignment. The numbers had been right, but the *chemistry* was wrong. I had trusted analysis over intuition.

Since then, I've learned to trust that quiet inner voice, the one that speaks not in panic but in peace. True discernment begins where noise ends.

And sometimes, the bravest decision isn't to act, it's to wait.

Listening Beyond Data

The modern leader is flooded with information, dashboards, reports, KPIs, feedback loops. We've built entire systems to ensure we never have to guess again. But data without discernment is like light without focus: bright, but blinding.

I once worked under a CEO who could quote data trends by memory but couldn't read the room. He led with spreadsheets instead of empathy.

The result? Brilliant strategies that failed in practice because they ignored the human pulse beneath the numbers.

Discernment doesn't reject data, it humanizes it. It asks the second question:

"What story is this data trying to tell me?"

For example, when staff turnover spikes, the obvious cause might be workload. But discernment listens deeper: Is it really workload, or is it the loss of meaning? Is it exhaustion, or erosion of trust?

In leadership, the most dangerous problems are rarely the visible ones, they're the emotional fractures we don't name because we're too busy measuring output.

In family life, it's the same. When a child withdraws or a spouse grows distant, we can rush to fix behavior instead of understanding emotion. Discernment invites us to slow down and *see beneath the symptom*.

The Courage to Wait
Every decision carries pressure, from timelines, boards, or expectations. The world demands speed, but wisdom often hides in delay.

I once was the Chair of a nonprofit whose board was divided over a major property purchase. Half wanted to expand; half feared overreach. The debate was heated, the urgency palpable. Everyone wanted resolution *now*.

I asked a simple question: "What if we waited a month?"

They stared at me as if I'd spoken heresy. But they agreed. That month of space revealed what adrenaline had hidden, that their growth model wasn't ready to sustain expansion. Waiting saved them millions.

We often mistake delay for indecision, but in truth, it's discipline.

The best leaders I know make peace with the discomfort of not yet knowing. They trust that clarity emerges not from haste, but from stillness.

There's an old saying in contemplative traditions: *"Don't just do something, sit there."*
It sounds counterintuitive, but it's deeply practical. The pause is where discernment gathers strength.

The Father's Lens
Discernment at home looks a little different, but it follows the same logic.

One night, after a long day, my teenage daughter came into the kitchen clearly upset. I could tell something had happened at school. My instinct was to fix it, to offer advice, to protect. But something told me to listen first.

So I sat down beside her, said nothing, and waited.
After a few minutes of silence, she began to talk, slowly at first, then with release. I realized she didn't want answers; she wanted presence.

That night, I learned again that discernment isn't about having the right response, it's about recognizing what's *needed*.

In leadership, as in fatherhood, our first impulse is often to solve. But discernment whispers, "Not yet." It asks us to trade reaction for relationship.

Noise and the Fear of Missing Out

The fear of missing out, FOMO, drives many of our worst decisions. It's the whisper that says, *If you don't act now, you'll fall behind.*

But discernment knows that real opportunities don't expire under pressure. They deepen under patience.

I once coached a young executive who said yes to every partnership, every project, every invitation. He was brilliant but burned out. One afternoon, I asked him to list his top five priorities for the year. He wrote down twelve.

We spent the next hour cutting them. Each time we crossed one out, he winced, until the list reached three.

When he looked at the final three, he said quietly, "These are the only ones that actually matter."

Six months later, his performance, and peace, had transformed. He hadn't lost influence; he'd gained integrity.

Discernment doesn't limit you, it liberates you from false urgency.

The Practice of Alignment

At its core, discernment is alignment, between who you are, what you value, and what you do.

When those three drift apart, burnout begins. When they realign, purpose returns.

I now begin every major decision, whether professional or personal, with three questions:

1. Does this align with our purpose?

2. Does this serve people or ego?

3. Does it create peace or pressure?

If I can answer "yes" to the first two and "peace" to the third, I move forward. If not, I pause.

It's astonishing how many crises vanish when you honor that kind of clarity.

The Wisdom of Limits

The poet Wendell Berry wrote, *"The mind that is not baffled is not employed. The impeded stream is the one that sings."*

Leadership will always carry complexity. But discernment transforms that complexity into song.
It teaches you to accept limits not as loss, but as design.

Every system, from an ecosystem to a business, thrives within boundaries. Trees grow taller not by escaping the soil, but by drawing from it.
In the same way, leaders and fathers grow deeper when they honor the limits that define their calling.

The question isn't, *How much can I hold?*
It's, *What is mine to hold?*

Self-Reflection

1. When was the last time you made a decision that looked right but felt wrong? What did that tension teach you?

2. Which commitments in your life might be "good things" that are blocking the *best things?*

3. Where are you being invited to wait, to listen, or to pause before acting?

Habits that Matter

- **The 3 A.M. Test:** Before finalizing any major decision, sit with it in stillness, away from noise, titles, and deadlines. Does peace or pressure remain?

- **Pattern Recognition:** Review your last five decisions that caused stress. What common thread or motivation underpinned them?

- **Alignment Review:** Create a short "values filter", three words that define your leadership essence (e.g., clarity, compassion, courage). Run every choice through them.

- **Family Parallel:** The next time conflict arises at home, resist advice. Ask instead, "What do you need most right now, a solution or someone to listen?

The Art of Saying No

It was a Wednesday afternoon when I first realized how profoundly a single word could change a life.

Not "yes," but *no*.

I was sitting in a small conference room, surrounded by the kind of energy that hums just before burnout, a whiteboard covered in ideas, a dozen ambitious voices competing for airtime, a calendar already overflowing. Everyone was eager to say yes to the next opportunity, the next initiative, the next "must-win battle."

As the discussion spiraled into enthusiasm and overwhelm, I caught my own reflection in the window, tired eyes, clenched jaw, that familiar weight behind the ribs. And I thought: *We are saying yes to everything because we're too afraid to say no to anything.*

So I did it. I raised my hand and said, "We're not ready. We need to stop."

The silence that followed was seismic. But in that silence, something sacred happened, clarity returned. The noise fell away, and purpose re-emerged.

That moment became a turning point in my leadership and in my life. Because learning to say no, gracefully, consistently, courageously, is not an act of resistance. It's an act of wisdom.

The Tyranny of Yes

From the moment we begin leading, or parenting, the world trains us to say yes.

Yes to opportunity.
Yes to urgency.
Yes to being needed.

It starts with good intentions, to help, to serve, to prove we can. But over time, yes becomes a reflex instead of a choice.

And here's the danger: every "yes" costs something. It draws energy, time, focus, often from the very things that matter most. Every time you say yes to something, you inevitably say no to something else.

Saying yes too easily turns leaders into human bottlenecks, overcommitted, overstretched, under-inspired. Families feel it too. Parents who can't say no to every demand become exhausted, distracted, and distant.

We confuse availability with love, responsiveness with care. But love, true, mature love, doesn't mean saying yes to everyone. It means saying yes to what gives life meaning.

The paradox is that when you try to be everything to everyone, you end up being *nothing to anyone.*

The No That Saved a Company
Years ago, I worked with a social enterprise that was expanding rapidly. Every week brought new proposals, partnerships, programs, pilot projects. The founder, a visionary with a huge heart, said yes to nearly all of them.

The early months were exhilarating, but within a year, the organization was struggling. Staff were overworked, donors confused, impact diluted.

In an emergency retreat, we gathered the leadership team and listed everything on the table, forty-seven active initiatives. The whiteboard looked like a mind map of chaos.

I asked a simple question: "If we could only keep five, which ones would they be?"

The room went quiet. One by one, we started erasing. It was painful, projects people had poured their hearts into disappeared under the marker. But as the clutter cleared, we could breathe again.

When we finished, the founder looked at the board, now clean except for five initiatives, and said softly, "That's who we are."

Within six months, the organization was thriving again. Not because we did more, but because we finally understood less is not loss, it's focus.

That day I learned something I never forgot:

Saying no doesn't close doors. It opens the right ones.

The Courage to Disappoint

Saying no feels dangerous because it invites disappointment. We fear letting people down, employees, partners, even family. We fear being seen as unhelpful, uncooperative, or weak.

But boundaries are not barriers; they're commitments to purpose.

Years ago, I walked out on a lucrative contracting role. It aligned with my skills but not my values. The organization's culture prized profit over people, efficiency over empathy. I knew staying would compromise something internal, that quiet compass I've learned to trust.

When I said no, I felt both terrified and free. The following week, another opportunity appeared, perfectly aligned with the work I wanted to do. That choice changed the trajectory of my career and saw me spend the next thirteen years in the Aged Care Industry – the best classroom and proving ground, I could have ever asked for.

I've seen the same truth play out in family life.

Once, my son begged me to coach his sports team. My schedule was impossible, but the guilt was strong. Everything in me wanted to say yes.

Instead, I told him the truth: "I can't coach this season, mate, but I'll be at every game. You'll see me there."

He nodded. And he did. Every week, on the sidelines, I watched, fully present, not multitasking, not half-engaged.

Months later, he said, "Dad, I'm glad you didn't coach. You got to be my dad, not the coach."

Sometimes saying no isn't rejection, it's refinement. It's choosing your true role over the one you feel pressured to fill.

Boundaries and the Brain

Neuroscience supports what wise leaders and parents have always known: our brains can't handle endless yeses. Every commitment, even small ones, consumes *cognitive bandwidth*, a limited resource that fuels decision-making, creativity, and empathy.

Psychologists call it decision fatigue, the erosion of clarity caused by too many choices. When everything matters, nothing does.

Saying no preserves energy for what's essential. It sharpens thought, strengthens empathy, and prevents burnout.

There's also a deeper psychological truth: every no reaffirms identity. It reminds us who we are and what we stand for. Boundaries, properly held, aren't walls that separate, they're the lines that define shape. Without them, we dissolve into obligation.

Leadership without boundaries becomes martyrdom. Parenthood without boundaries becomes exhaustion.

Boundaries are the structure of love.

The Polite No

The art of saying no lies not in the word itself, but in *how* it's said.

A "no" can wound or it can liberate. It can shut down relationship or deepen respect.

Over the years, I've refined my approach into three simple steps:

1. **Affirm the value.** Acknowledge the importance of what's being asked. ("I really appreciate you thinking of me for this project.")

2. **Be honest and brief.** No long justifications, no apologies. ("I can't commit to that right now.")

3. **Offer alignment.** If possible, suggest another way to contribute or connect. ("Let's revisit this in a few months," or "I know someone who might be a better fit.")

A gracious no communicates confidence, not coldness. It tells others you know your priorities, and you respect theirs.

I once heard Brené Brown put it perfectly: *"Clear is kind."* Clarity, even when it disappoints, is more compassionate than overpromising and underdelivering.

The Father's Parallel

One evening, my teenage daughter asked to attend a party I wasn't comfortable with. Every fiber of me wanted to avoid the argument, to say yes and keep the peace. But I knew the situation wasn't right.

When I said no, she stormed off, doors slammed, tears flowed. I sat in the quiet afterwards, questioning myself. Had I been too strict? Too cautious?

A week later, we found out the party had been broken up by police. She came into the kitchen, eyes wet but softer this time, and said, "Thanks, Dad."

It wasn't victory, it was validation. The kind that comes not from being right, but from being rooted.

Leadership, like parenting, requires the courage to be temporarily unpopular.
Sometimes love wears the face of restraint.

The Spiritual Dimension of No

There's something almost sacred about restraint. It's woven into the fabric of creation itself, boundaries between light and dark, sea and shore, day and night.

The power of a boundary is that it defines where flourishing happens. Every yes without a no erodes that boundary. It blurs purpose.

In faith traditions across centuries, "no" has always been tied to freedom. The Sabbath itself is a divine no, a refusal to work, to hurry, to strive. It's the weekly reminder that doing less can be an act of worship.

In that same spirit, saying no to excess, ego, or distraction is not deprivation. It's devotion, to what truly matters, to the people entrusted to your care, to the inner life that sustains your outer impact.

Learning to Trust the Consequence

Not every no will be understood. Some will cost relationships, opportunities, comfort. But leadership rooted in discernment doesn't chase approval; it seeks alignment.

I've had to decline new roles, invitations, even friendships that pulled me away from the path I was called to walk. It wasn't easy. Some people left quietly. Others left loudly.
But over time, the right people stayed, the ones who valued purpose over proximity.

Each no clarified not just my calendar, but my character. And with every no, the remaining yeses grew deeper.

Self-Reflection

- What recent "yes" do you regret, and what might a healthy no have preserved?

- Who are you afraid to disappoint, and why?

- What would your leadership or family life look like if every yes had to pass through the filter of purpose and peace?

Habits that Matter

- **The 72-Hour Rule:** When presented with a new request or opportunity, wait three days before replying. Urgency fades; clarity grows.

- **The "Yes Budget":** Decide in advance how many major commitments you can sustain each quarter. Guard it like a financial budget.

- **The Family Filter:** For one month, limit family activities to what brings joy or connection. Let go of everything else and observe how the household tone shifts.

- **Graceful Decline Practice:** Write a short "no" response for three scenarios, one personal, one professional, one relational. Keep them honest and kind.

Doing Less, Better

There's a photograph I keep on my office shelf, black and white, slightly faded. It shows a craftsman in his workshop, his hands steady over a single piece of wood. You can see, in the lines of his face and the quiet tension in his shoulders, that he's been at this for decades. There's no rush in him. Only rhythm. Only care.

Every time I glance at that photograph, I'm reminded of a truth our culture has almost forgotten: excellence isn't born from doing more, it's born from doing *less, better*.

The craftsman doesn't hurry. He doesn't multitask. He knows that mastery requires margin, that quality requires patience. His work will take as long as it takes, and because of that, it will last longer than the things made in haste.

Leadership and fatherhood are the same.

Doing less, better, isn't a tactic. It's a philosophy. It's the belief that depth is greater than breadth, that a smaller circle of focus can hold far more meaning than a sprawling empire of distraction.

The Productivity Trap

Modern leaders live in a paradox. We have more tools for productivity than any generation before us, yet most of us feel less productive than ever.

Our devices promise efficiency but deliver exhaustion. We respond faster, but think shallower. We fill calendars with meetings, and our minds with metrics, until there's no room left for imagination or insight.

I once sat with an executive whose calendar was so overbooked that his assistant color-coded the chaos. Twenty-seven meetings a week. Four hundred unread emails. His business card could have listed "professional responder" as his title.

When I asked how he felt, he said, "I'm busy, but I'm not moving."

That phrase haunted me - *Busy, but not moving.*

He wasn't lazy. He was lost, trapped in a loop of reaction, mistaking motion for progress. It took months of disciplined restructuring, cancelling standing meetings, consolidating projects, redistributing authority, before he rediscovered what focus felt like.

When we finally sat down after the shift, he smiled and said, "I feel like a leader again, not a manager of chaos."

That's what doing less, better, does. It restores you to yourself.

Depth Over Breadth

When I was younger, I wanted my leadership to be expansive, to touch everything, influence everyone. I chased scale. But over time, I've come to see that greatness doesn't spread outward; it grows *downward*.

In families, that truth is easy to see. Children don't need parents who do everything. They need parents who do *a few things well and consistently*. Presence. Listening. Stability.
A few deep roots will hold a tree through any storm.

In organizations, the same law applies. The most resilient companies don't chase every market; they build a core so strong that expansion becomes organic. Apple under Steve Jobs was famous for killing projects. When he returned to the company in 1997, he reduced their product line from 350 to 10. It wasn't minimalism, it was mastery.

Jobs once said, "I'm as proud of what we don't do as I am of what we do."

That line could hang above the doorway of every great leader and every wise parent.

Doing less, better, means embracing boundaries as creative fuel, saying, *This is enough, and within it, I will make something extraordinary.*

The Myth of the Multitasker

For years, I believed I could outpace limits. I prided myself on juggling, answering messages between meetings, reviewing reports while eating dinner, drafting strategies in airport lounges.

But science tells us what experience eventually confirms: multitasking isn't productivity. It's task-switching, and every switch costs time, focus, and empathy.

Neuroscientists estimate that shifting between tasks can reduce efficiency by up to 40%. Worse, it trains the brain to live in perpetual distraction.

The real casualty of multitasking, though, isn't efficiency, it's connection.
When you're half-present, people feel it. They may not call it out, but they register it as absence.

At home, I saw this with painful clarity. My daughter once said, "Dad, can you look at me when I talk to you?" I realized I'd been listening with my ears but not my eyes, answering while glancing at my phone.

Doing less, better, often begins with the humbling acknowledgment that we've been living half-aware.

The good news? Awareness is the first step toward restoration.

The Quiet Power of Focus

In 1956, psychologist George Miller proposed what became known as *Miller's Law*, the idea that the average person can hold about seven things in working memory at once. That limit hasn't changed, despite our technology. We can manage more information, but we can't *meaningfully attend* to more things at once.

Focus, therefore, is a superpower, not because it's rare, but because it's protected.

I often ask leaders in workshops:
"What would change if you gave your best attention to only three things this quarter?"

The responses are always the same: relief, possibility, clarity.

We underestimate how much momentum is hidden inside focus. When a leader defines three clear priorities, the entire organization exhales. Teams know what matters, people align, energy concentrates.

In families, the same is true. When you strip away the clutter of overcommitment, too many activities, too many plans, you make room for joy to return.

Focus is love made visible. It's the decision to pour yourself fully into the few things that hold your deepest purpose.

The Father's Workshop

A few years ago, a friend of mine built a small workshop behind his house, a humble shed really, with a bench, some tools, and the smell of fresh cut pine in the air. It was built for pace, not for productivity.

One afternoon, his youngest daughter wandered in while he was sanding a board. She watched for a while and then asked, "Why do you do it so slowly?"

He smiled and said, "Because if I rush, I ruin it."

She nodded, then stayed to help, carefully, attentively, quietly.

They finished one small project that day, but he learned something much larger: Children, and teams, don't just learn from what we *produce*. They learn from how we *proceed*.

Doing less, better, isn't about efficiency; it's about modeling peace. It teaches others that worth isn't measured in output but in *how we bring ourselves to the work.*

Excellence as Love
There's a quiet holiness in excellence, not perfectionism, but care.

When you do less, better, you offer the world your attention as a gift. And attention, in any form, is an expression of love.

The writer Annie Dillard once said, "How we spend our days is, of course, how we spend our lives."

Doing less, better, ensures that those days are not squandered in noise.

Another version states, "How we do anything, is how we do everything"

I've watched teams rediscover joy when freed from overload. I've seen fathers rebuild trust simply by showing up undistracted. The common thread is the same, depth heals what busyness breaks.

When excellence flows from love rather than ego, it becomes a legacy rather than a performance.

The Discipline of Completion

One of the most underrated skills in leadership is *finishing*. We start endlessly, new projects, new goals, new plans, but completion requires courage. It demands saying, "This is enough."

I once witnessed a team that struggled with follow-through. They were brilliant at beginnings but scattered at endings. So they made a rule: nothing new until something old was complete.

At first, the room groaned. But within months, morale improved. Energy returned.

Why? Because completion brings dignity. It restores momentum and confidence.

Families need the same discipline. We often chase new goals, holidays, renovations, activities, without finishing the simpler commitments that matter more. Sometimes, the bravest act of love is to finish a conversation, a promise, or an apology.

Doing less, better, honors the dignity of the finish line.

Doing Less as Resistance

In a culture addicted to acceleration, doing less is an act of quiet rebellion.

It says, "I refuse to measure my worth by my output."

When you slow down enough to think deeply, create carefully, or rest deliberately, you're challenging a world that equates value with volume.

It's not laziness. It's leadership, the kind that knows transformation never happens in haste.

History's greatest movements, from social change to spiritual renewal, didn't emerge from frenzy; they were birthed in reflection, contemplation, and courage to act with clarity.

To do less, better, is to move with the grain of wisdom itself.

Self-Reflection

1. What area of your life feels overcomplicated, where too many commitments have diluted excellence?

2. What would it look like to trade quantity for quality in your leadership, work, or home life?

3. Which unfinished promise or project needs your full attention before you move to something new?

Habits that Matter

- **The Rule of Three:** Choose three priorities for the week. Protect them fiercely. Let everything else orbit around them.

- **The Completion Habit:** Finish one meaningful task each day before starting another. Small completions restore confidence.

- **Unplugged Excellence:** For one day each month, work or create without devices. Notice how focus transforms your output.

- **Family Simplicity Challenge:** Cancel one recurring obligation this month, a meeting, activity, or routine, and use that space for shared rest or play.

The Paradox of Priority

It's a quiet Friday evening. The week has finally exhaled. I'm staring out the back window, watching the sky soften into that slow Australian twilight, magpies warbling, air cooling, the faint smell of rain in the distance. My phone buzzes once on the table beside me, then again, then again. Messages. Notifications. Invitations to re-enter the noise.

For a moment, I reach toward it, instinctively, habitually, then stop. I take a breath and let it ring into silence.

It's in moments like this that I realize something both humbling and liberating: The world will keep spinning without me.

It always does.

That truth is at the heart of what I've come to call the paradox of priority, the idea that by doing *less*, we actually become *more effective, more peaceful, more human*. That narrowing our focus expands our influence. That slowing down allows everything meaningful to accelerate.

Priorities form the second pillar of FatherFramed™ Leadership, the discipline of choosing what matters most so you can lead with clarity instead of chaos. Without this, both homes and workplaces drift into noise.

It sounds counterintuitive in a culture built on the velocity of ambition. But every great leader, every grounded parent, every wise soul I've met has discovered the same hidden law: when you give yourself wholly to the few things that matter most, everything else starts to fall into place.

The Weight of Infinite Options

Modern life has given us infinite access, to information, to opportunity, to choice. Yet with it has come a deep, quiet anxiety.

Psychologists call it *decision overload*. The more options we have, the harder it becomes to discern meaning.

Leaders feel this pressure acutely. Every day brings more decisions than the mind was designed to process, about people, policies, priorities, profits. Every "yes" adds invisible weight. Over time, those yeses stack until even the most capable leaders feel hollowed out.

At home, it's the same. The constant scheduling, the pursuit of enrichment, the subtle competition to do more and be more, it erodes the peace that family is meant to bring.

Somewhere along the way, we stopped asking, "What's enough?"

The paradox is this: success gives you more opportunities than you can handle. Wisdom gives you permission to decline them.

The Geometry of Focus

I once heard focus described as "the shape of purpose." Without it, our energy diffuses; with it, our lives take form.

I learned this truth through failure.

Early in my leadership career, I ran a team in an organization that was growing fast, new locations, new hires, new expectations. Growth felt like progress, so I kept saying yes. But as we scaled wider, we thinned out. Quality slipped. Culture frayed.

One night, reviewing reports well past midnight, I realized I'd lost sight of what had made us great in the first place: care, connection, community. We had expanded the structure but hollowed the soul.

So, I did something that startled my CEO, I proposed we pause expansion for a year. We called it *The Year of Better Before Bigger*.

We focused inward, refining our systems, training our people, repairing our foundations. It wasn't glamorous. But it was transformative.

Within twelve months, revenue stabilized, morale surged, and trust returned. When we eventually grew again, it was sustainable, because it was rooted.

As S. Truett Cathy stated at Chic-fil-A "We must become better before we are bigger, then our customers will demand we become bigger"

The geometry of focus is like that, it narrows before it expands.

The Lie of Balance

We're told constantly to "find balance", between work and life, ambition and rest, self and service. But balance, as most people define it, is a myth.

Balance implies equal weight, as if every area of life deserves identical attention. But life doesn't work that way. The seasons aren't equal. The tides don't hold still.

Priority isn't balance; it's rhythm.

Some seasons demand intensity, launching a business, raising toddlers, leading through crisis. Others invite restoration, reflection, reconnection, renewal.

The wisdom lies not in balancing all things at once, but in knowing which season you're in and living it fully.

As a younger leader, I tried to do everything simultaneously, scale the organization, deepen my marriage, raise children, stay fit, volunteer, read, rest. The result was predictable: I did all of it, badly.

Eventually, I realized the truth, you can do *anything* for a season, but not *everything* at once.

So now, I lead by rhythm, not rigidity. Some weeks demand more from my professional life; others pull me toward home. The goal isn't symmetry. It's sincerity, to be wherever I am, fully.

Presence, not balance, is what brings peace.

The Cost of Clarity

Clarity always comes at a cost, especially in leadership. When you choose a few priorities, you will inevitably disappoint someone.

You will say no to opportunities that others call "essential." You will choose focus over popularity, discipline over applause. And that's uncomfortable, sometimes painfully so.

But if you don't set your own priorities, the world will assign them for you.

Years ago, when I was still learning this lesson, I took a phone call during a family dinner, "just this once," I told myself. My son was in the middle of telling a story, and when I came back to the table, he had stopped talking. The look on his face said everything.

That night, I wrote down a phrase I've never forgotten:

"Every yes to the world is a no to someone at home."

I don't always get it right. But every time I remember that sentence, I recalibrate. It's my internal compass, pointing me back to the quiet, unseen commitments that matter most.

Priorities aren't schedules. They're values in action.

Saying Yes to the Right Things

Prioritization isn't about saying no forever. It's about saying *yes with integrity.*

When I finally understood this, my leadership became lighter, and sharper. I began asking two questions before any major decision:

1. *Does this align with my purpose?*

2. *Can I give it my best attention without betraying what I already value?*

If the answer to either was no, I passed.

The paradox is that my influence grew as my commitments shrank. Fewer projects, deeper impact. Fewer meetings, stronger relationships. Fewer ambitions, greater peace.

At home, it looked the same. I said no to weekend commitments to say yes to Saturday pancakes, to family walks, to unstructured conversations. And slowly, the joy that had been suffocated by busyness began to breathe again.

It's not the size of your yes that defines your life. It's the *substance* of it.

When Doing Less Becomes Leadership

Leadership used to mean control, being across every detail, every decision. But in the new economy of trust and autonomy, leadership means *creating space.*

Space for people to think.
Space for teams to grow.
Space for ideas to emerge that aren't yours.

Doing less as a leader is an act of humility. It says, "I don't need to be the center."

One of my proudest leadership moments came not from something I did, but something I *didn't* do. A team I'd mentored for years presented a new initiative. Normally, I would have offered feedback or adjustments. Instead, I listened, asked questions, and simply said, "I trust you. Run with it."

They did. It succeeded beyond expectation. Later, one of them said, "It felt different, like you believed we could do it without you."

That's when I realized the paradox of priority isn't just about time, it's about ego. When you prioritize what truly matters, you release your need to control everything else.

True leadership is the art of *doing less so others can do more.*

The Father's Perspective
My children are growing older now, one in university, one finished school, one still at school, and the youngest one who is now the tallest in the family.

The seasons of parenting, like leadership, have their own paradoxes. When they were small, they needed my constant attention. Now they need my restraint, my ability to step back, to listen more than direct, to let them fail safely and rise stronger.

It's taken me years to learn that love matures as it simplifies. When they were young, love was expressed in doing: building, teaching, protecting. Now it's expressed in being: presence, patience, prayer.

The same transformation happens in great leaders. In youth, we prove ourselves through activity. In maturity, we prove ourselves through restraint.

The Peace of Enough

There's a moment, and if you haven't had it yet, it will come, when you realize that the life you've been striving to build is already here. It doesn't need expansion; it needs attention.

The peace of enough is the quiet end of ambition's fever. It doesn't kill drive, it purifies it. It turns achievement into gratitude, performance into purpose.

I've stood in boardrooms after massive wins and felt empty, and I've sat at a simple family dinner, laughter spilling across the table, and felt rich beyond measure.

The world may not reward simplicity, but it always respects mastery. And mastery, in leadership, in love, in life, is nothing more than disciplined devotion to the few things that truly matter.

Self-Reflection

1. What does "enough" look like for you, in work, family, and personal growth?

2. Which priorities have drifted from alignment with your deepest values?

3. What would your life feel like if you measured success not by more, but by peace?

Habits that Matter

- **The Alignment Review:** Write down your top five priorities. Then circle only three. The circled ones define your next season.

- **The Sabbath Principle:** Designate one day or evening each week for complete rest, no work, no planning. Protect it fiercely.

- **The Exit Audit:** For every new commitment you add, remove one. Keep the ecosystem of your life balanced.

- **The Gratitude Check:** Each night, name one small thing that mattered most today, and one thing that didn't. Let go of the latter before sleep.

Closing Thought

In the end, priorities are not about productivity, they're about peace.

They are how we choose to spend the finite currency of our lives.

To lead like a father is to know when to act and when to rest, when to strive and when to surrender, when to chase the horizon and when to stay home by the fire.

Doing less, better, is not about efficiency.
It's about eternity, about making room for what will last when everything else fades.

Priorities form the second pillar of the FatherFrame™, the discipline that turns intention into clarity and clarity into integrity.

"What matters most," I've come to believe, "was never the scale of our impact, but the sincerity of our attention."

Once you reclaim clarity around what truly deserves your energy, the way you express that clarity becomes your next act of leadership. Priorities without communication create frustration; communication without priorities creates noise.

The people you lead cannot follow what they cannot hear and they cannot hear what you have not yet named. With your attention centered and your choices refined, the next chapter explores how communication becomes the language of trust, the bridge between intention and understanding, and the heartbeat of every relationship you hope to strengthen.

Chapter Three – Communication: The Language of Trust

"Words shape worlds. How you listen, speak, and frame meaning determines whether people feel understood, valued, and aligned with purpose."

Communication is more than transmitting information, it is the daily construction of trust. How you listen, the tone you use, and the way you shape meaning creates a sense of belonging or distance, clarity or confusion.

This chapter shows how communication mirrors fatherhood: the words you choose can steady someone, empower them, or help them see themselves differently. When leaders communicate with intention, empathy, and courage, teams become safer, more aligned, and more motivated. Great communication is not a skill; it's a leadership identity.

Communication is another anchor within the FatherFramed™ Leadership Model, the way presence and priorities take shape in language. How we speak, listen, and frame meaning becomes the daily architecture of trust.

The Sound of Trust

There's a sound I'll never forget, my father's voice when he said my name.

It wasn't loud. It didn't have to be. There was something in the tone, a blend of steadiness and warmth, that made you want to listen. Even now, years later, I can still hear it in my head when I need to make a difficult decision or steady myself before a meeting.

He didn't use many words, but the ones he did carried weight. They felt like anchors, gentle, grounding, real.

And that's the paradox of communication: we spend most of our lives trying to be heard, when the true power lies in how we make others *feel* when we speak.

Communication becomes leadership when your words create clarity, your listening creates belonging, and your tone creates trust.

The Foundation Beneath Every Word

Communication is the bloodstream of leadership, the oxygen of relationship. Yet for all our speaking, we are often starving for connection.

In the modern workplace, messages move faster than meaning.

We have emails, text messages, voice memos, Teams Calls, Zoom, channels multiplying by the hour, and yet, trust remains fragile.

Why? Because communication has become transactional. We speak to *transfer information* rather than to *build understanding*.

The leaders I've admired most were not the most articulate, but the most authentic. They had a way of speaking that made you feel both seen and safe. They weren't performing; they were present.

Their words didn't just inform, they *transformed*.

I once worked under a CEO who rarely gave speeches. But when he did, the room quieted, not because of charisma, but because of *calm*.

He spoke slowly, never with notes. You could feel that every word had been earned through reflection, not rehearsed for approval.

When he said, "We'll get through this together," no one doubted him. It wasn't a slogan, it was a promise.

That's what trust sounds like.

The Frequency of Presence
In every conversation, whether at home, in the boardroom, or office corridor, there's an invisible frequency, the energy of presence.

You can hear it in someone's tone, see it in their eyes, feel it in the way they pause before replying. Presence is the language beneath the language, the unspoken current that shapes every exchange.

Think about the last time you spoke with someone who wasn't truly there. Their eyes darted, their responses were delayed or polite but hollow. The conversation technically happened, but connection didn't.

Now remember the opposite, when someone listened so fully that you forgot your rehearsed words and spoke from your heart. That's the power of presence in communication.

In families, this is everything. Children, especially, have a radar for divided attention. They may not articulate it, but they feel when your mind is elsewhere.

I once read a study showing that when parents are distracted by phones during conversations with their kids, the children mirror that disconnection later, becoming less responsive and more withdrawn. The message isn't just "you're busy." It's "I'm not worth your full attention."

In leadership, the same wound appears. Teams that don't feel heard stop speaking truth. Silence becomes self-preservation. And once that happens, innovation dies.

Presence builds trust because it communicates something deeper than competence: *care*.

The Unspoken Contract
Every relationship, professional or personal, is held together by an unspoken contract:

"I will treat your words as sacred, and you will do the same with mine."

Break that contract once, and you might recover. Break it repeatedly, and no amount of eloquence can restore trust.

I've seen leaders lose entire teams not because of one wrong decision, but because they failed to mean what they said. They spoke promises into the air and never followed through.

Words without consistency are like currency without backing, they lose value.

In my own leadership, I've made this mistake more than once. In the rush of enthusiasm, I've overpromised, not out of deceit, but out of optimism. Yet to those on the receiving end, the impact is the same: hope deferred.

Now I try to practice a discipline I call *verbal integrity*, never saying what I don't intend to sustain. It's harder than it sounds. It means pausing before every "yes," being willing to say "I don't know," and admitting when I was wrong sooner rather than later.

It's humbling, but it's humanizing.

And in a world drowning in spin and noise, honesty feels revolutionary.

When Words Heal
There's a power in language that extends beyond logic, it shapes emotion, memory, even physiology.

Research from UCLA neuroscientist Matthew Lieberman showed that simply *naming* emotions, saying "I feel angry," "I feel anxious,", reduces the brain's amygdala response, calming fear. It's called *affect labelling*.

I've seen this in boardrooms and kitchens alike.
When conflict brews, the person who can put words to the tension without blame changes the atmosphere.

"I sense frustration."
"I hear your disappointment."
"I think I made a mistake."
"I feel like this is a test."

Those simple phrases disarm defensiveness. They invite truth instead of resistance.

I remember a moment, years ago with a colleague who'd been underperforming. The easy path would have been criticism. Instead, I began with, "I think we've both been running so hard that we stopped understanding each other."

He exhaled, visibly. We ended the conversation not with blame, but with a plan.

At home, it's the same miracle in miniature. The right words at the right moment can restore harmony faster than a thousand lectures.

Once, after a heated family argument, I sat down beside my daughter, still fuming. Instead of defending myself, I said quietly, "You matter more to me than being right."

Her anger melted. Mine did too.

That's the sound of trust, not the absence of conflict, but the presence of care stronger than ego.

Self-Reflection

1. When you speak, at work or at home, do your words connect, or just communicate?

2. Where in your life has trust been weakened by inconsistency between what's said and what's done?

3. What tone of voice do you want people to remember you by?

Habits that Matter

- **The 3-Second Pause:** Before responding in conversation, wait three seconds. It signals attentiveness and prevents reaction.

- **Tone Audit:** Ask someone you trust how your communication makes them *feel*. Don't defend, just listen.

- **Follow-Through Rule:** Don't say "I'll get back to you" unless you mean it. Build verbal reliability one promise at a time.

- **Family Parallel:** Spend ten minutes each day in undistracted conversation with your child or partner. Ask, "How was your day?" and listen without advice.

The Weight of Words

There are few things in the world more powerful than language, and few things we use with less awareness.

Every civilization, every culture, every movement begins with words. They name reality, define belonging, inspire courage, or ignite destruction. They build homes and burn them down.

Leadership, like fatherhood, begins in speech, not in command, but in tone.

The way we speak, day after day, becomes the atmosphere others live in.

Words have the power of life and death, and I often think of words like seeds: easy to scatter, slow to grow, impossible to take back once they've taken root.

The Architecture of Culture

If you want to know what a culture truly values, listen to how it speaks.

Every workplace, family, or community has a shared language, often invisible to those within it. Some speak in encouragement; others in cynicism. Some in clarity; others in coded tension.

Culture is not built by slogans on walls; it's built by sentences in hallways.

Years ago, I visited a retail organization with one of the healthiest cultures I'd ever seen. People smiled genuinely. Meetings ended on time. Accountability was mutual, not managerial.

When I asked the CEO how they'd built it, she said, "We changed our words."

She showed me their internal lexicon, the small linguistic shifts that had redefined their daily interactions. "Problems" became "learning opportunities." "Staff" became "team." "Targets" became "commitments."

The transformation wasn't superficial; it was psychological.

Language isn't just expression; it's *creation*. The words we repeat shape what we believe. Over time, those beliefs harden into culture.

In family life, the same dynamic holds true. The tone we set, the language of criticism or compassion, blame or blessing, becomes the emotional climate our children grow up in.

A child raised on words of patience learns to trust.
A child raised on words of sharpness learns to hide.

The home and the workplace share this sacred truth: you can't speak poison and expect peace to grow.

The Neuroscience of Tone

Science now confirms what intuition has always known, our tone of voice has physiological impact.

When we speak harshly, the listener's brain registers it as threat. The amygdala, the brain's emotional alarm system, triggers cortisol and adrenaline. Even mild sarcasm can cause a stress response.

Conversely, calm, affirming tones activate the vagus nerve, the body's relaxation pathway. Heart rate steadies, oxygen intake improves, and the brain opens to collaboration and creativity.

Tone, in other words, determines whether people feel safe or defensive.

A leader's voice sets the emotional baseline for a team. A father's voice sets the emotional baseline for a home.

I've felt this in my own life. On rushed mornings when my voice sharpens, I can see my children withdraw slightly, even if my words are reasonable. On other days, when I speak softly and slow down, the same message lands differently: received, not resisted.

Communication isn't just *what* we say; it's *how our nervous systems speak to each other.*

That's why great communicators are almost always self-regulated people. They've mastered their tone before they master their message.

The Leader's Echo

In leadership, every word echoes farther than you think.

A comment you make in passing can ripple through an organization for months. A careless joke can fracture trust. A moment of empathy can transform morale.

One of my mentors once said, "As a leader, you never have a neutral moment. Every sentence is either building trust or burning it."

That truth used to exhaust me, until I realized it wasn't a burden; it was an invitation to mindfulness.

Now, I speak with what I call "echo awareness." I ask myself, *How will this sound repeated in someone else's mouth tomorrow?*

If it would sound cynical, cruel, or unclear, I rephrase.

That habit has saved me from countless misunderstandings, and, just as importantly, has helped me see communication as stewardship, not performance.

Your words outlive your intentions. So make them kind enough to survive misinterpretation.

The Moral Responsibility of Speech
The older I get, the more I believe that speech carries moral weight.

Every word we release either affirms life or diminishes it.

We see this daily in leadership. Words can motivate teams through crisis, or humiliate them beyond repair. They can clarify vision, or destroy it in a single careless comment.

In faith traditions, words are sacred because they mirror creation itself: *"And God said, 'Let there be light.'"*

The act of speaking shaped the world.

In the secular sense, the principle still holds. When we speak, we participate in creation, shaping perception, identity, and possibility.

This is why gossip is so corrosive. It creates false worlds, imagined versions of people who must then live under that shadow. It's why public shaming, whether in an office or online, wounds collective trust.

Leadership is, in essence, public speech. And every public word carries private consequence.

The same applies at home. The way we speak to our children becomes the way they speak to themselves.

Tell a child they're lazy often enough, and they'll internalize it as identity. Tell them they're capable, and they'll rise to meet your faith.

Words don't just describe people. They *define* them.

That's why one of the most sacred duties of leadership, and fatherhood, is restraint.

Say less. Mean more.

When Words Become Healing Work

There's a kind of speech that doesn't just convey information, it restores dignity.

I remember visiting a workplace after a round of painful redundancies. Morale was low. Trust was fragile. The new manager began the first staff meeting not with strategy, but with confession.

She said, "I know this has been a season of loss. I can't pretend to have all the answers, but I want to say this clearly: you're not invisible to me. We're going to rebuild this, and we'll do it together."

No buzzwords. No polished slide deck. Just honesty, presence, and hope.

By the end of the week, people were volunteering ideas again. Energy returned.
Why? Because truth had spoken safety back into the room.

Words can reopen closed hearts. They can stitch trust where leadership has torn it.

The same principle applies at home. I've sat on the edge of my child's bed after an argument, unsure of what to say, then whispered, "I love you, even when I get it wrong."

That sentence has healed more than any lecture I've ever given.

The Daily Practice of Careful Speech

In the world of leadership, communication is often treated as a skill to refine. But in reality, it's a practice to sanctify, something to be done *carefully, deliberately, kindly,* every day.

Before important meetings, I take a moment to breathe and remind myself:

"What I say next will become someone else's memory."

That simple truth changes everything. It makes me speak slower, listen longer, and weigh every word with the gravity it deserves.

Words can't always fix what's broken, but they can begin the repair.

Self-Reflection

1. What words do people most associate with your leadership voice, reassuring, hurried, demanding, or calm?

2. When was the last time your tone betrayed your intention?

3. What language patterns (at home or work) do you want to consciously change to foster trust?

Habits that Matter

- **Tone Reset:** Before entering any meeting or family conversation, take one deep breath and ask, "How do I want them to *feel* after this?"

- **Vocabulary Audit:** Replace one habitual negative phrase ("problem," "issue," "failure") with a constructive one ("challenge," "lesson," "opportunity").

- **Echo Check:** When giving feedback, imagine it being repeated to you. Would you still feel respected?

- **Evening Repair:** Each night, reflect on one conversation you wish you'd handled better. Visualize how you'd phrase it tomorrow.

Listening for What's Not Said

We were once asked, "How many of you consider yourselves good listeners?" Nearly every hand went up.

Then asked, "How many of your teams would agree with you?" The room fell silent.

That silence said more than any survey could.

We like to believe we listen well, after all, we hear words all day. But hearing and listening are not the same thing. Hearing is physiological. Listening is *spiritual*. It requires stillness, humility, and the courage to let another person's truth rearrange yours.

It's no exaggeration to say that listening is the most underrated superpower in leadership, and the most profound act of love in fatherhood.

Because when you truly listen, you are doing something sacred: you are saying, *I will make space for your soul.*

The Discipline of Quiet

There's a story about a young monk who asked his teacher, "How can I learn to hear the divine?"

The teacher smiled and said, "Listen to the silence between the sounds."

That's where listening begins, not in the noise, but in the quiet between words.

In our age of perpetual communication, silence has become uncomfortable. We rush to fill it, with explanations, advice, and reassurance. But silence isn't emptiness; it's presence in its purest form.

When I first became a manager, I believed my job in conversations was to *respond*. To offer solutions, to fill the gaps. I thought that's what people wanted, answers. But most people don't want answers. They want acknowledgment. They want to be understood.

I learned this lesson one day during a difficult feedback session with a team member. He began explaining why he felt unseen, unappreciated. My instinct was to defend myself, to correct the record, to clarify. But something in me whispered, *Wait*.

So I did. I just listened.

When he finished, he looked down, then back up and said, "Thank you for not interrupting."

That moment transformed our relationship. I hadn't fixed anything. I'd simply created space, and that space was healing.

Listening is not passive. It's patient strength.

The Neuroscience of Empathy
Modern neuroscience confirms what the ancients understood intuitively: when we truly listen, our brains begin to mirror each other.

Functional MRI studies show that in moments of deep listening, the listener's neural activity synchronizes with the speaker's, a phenomenon called *interpersonal resonance*. It's the biological foundation of empathy.

That's why when someone listens to you deeply, you feel lighter. It's not imagination; it's chemistry. Your nervous system relaxes because you're no longer alone in your experience.

But here's the twist: true empathy requires self-regulation.
If your mind is racing, your empathy circuitry shuts down. If you're

preparing your next rebuttal while someone's talking, your brain can't attune to theirs.

That's why listening begins with slowing yourself down. You can't hear another's heart when yours is sprinting.

I've heard leaders in training repeat over and over: *"If you can't quiet your mind, you'll never hear the truth beneath the words."*

Empathy is not about agreement; it's about attunement, being so present that another person feels safe enough to be honest.

Listening Between the Lines

Every conversation has two layers, the *surface* of words and the *subtext* of emotion. Most leaders hear the former and miss the latter.

A team member says, "I'm fine," but her tone carries fatigue.
A partner says, "Do what you think is best," but their body tenses ever so slightly.
A child says, "It's not a big deal," but their eyes tell you it is.

The art of listening for what's not told lies in attending to the whole person, words, tone, expression, energy.

Once, during an executive meeting, a colleague vehemently opposed an idea I presented. His arguments were sharp, his voice rising. I could have countered point for point, but something in his face caught me, fear, not anger.

After the meeting, I asked quietly, "What's this really about for you?" He hesitated, then admitted, "I'm scared this change means I'm no longer needed. I'm worried about how it will affect me and my role"

Everything softened. We didn't just solve a policy issue, we restored trust.

That's what happens when you listen past resistance into vulnerability. Most conflict hides fear. Most silence hides longing.

Listening is the bridge that brings both safely into light.

The Father's Gift of Silence

Parenting taught me more about listening than any leadership course ever could.

Children don't always articulate what they need, especially as they grow older. They speak in sighs, in moods, in quiet changes of behavior. The temptation is to chase them with words, to fill the void with advice. But advice often lands like noise when the heart needs space.

One evening, my teenage daughter came home upset. She brushed past me, went straight to her room, and shut the door. I wanted to follow, to ask, to fix, but I didn't. I waited.

An hour later, she came out and sat beside me on the couch. Neither of us spoke. Eventually, she leaned her head on my shoulder and said softly, "I know you like to fix everything, but thanks for just being present."

That's when I realized: listening is sometimes the absence of words.

The same is true in leadership. Teams don't always need immediate answers. Sometimes they need to know that their leader can sit with uncertainty without panic.

The gift of silence communicates more than eloquence ever could. It says, *I trust that your truth matters enough to wait for it.*

The Humility to Learn

Listening also requires humility, the willingness to be changed by what you hear.

Most of us listen to confirm, not to learn. We enter conversations armed with conclusions, waiting for a pause long enough to insert our view. That's not listening; that's polite debate.

Humility transforms listening into dialogue. It allows for mutual discovery, a shared unfolding of truth neither person owned at the start.

In organizations, this humility builds cultures of innovation. When people know their voices genuinely shape direction, creativity flourishes.

In families, it builds belonging. When children realize their opinions are taken seriously, they grow into adults who believe their voices matter.

Listening, then, is not a soft skill. It's a justice skill. It restores equality where hierarchy could easily dominate.

Hearing the Heartbeat of an Organization
Every team, like every family, has a collective heartbeat, a rhythm of morale, energy, and emotion.

The leader's job is to keep a finger on that pulse.

You can measure KPIs and profits, but you can't manage what you don't *feel*. That's where deep listening becomes a diagnostic tool.

I've walked into workplaces where the air itself felt heavy, not from conflict, but from *unspokenness*. Conversations avoided. Feedback withheld. Meetings that ended with polite agreement and private frustration.

Silence in organizations is rarely peaceful; it's often protective. And it takes one courageous listener to break that pattern.

A single genuine question, "How are you really?", can change an entire culture, if it's asked with sincerity and followed by quiet attention.

Listening as Love

In the end, all communication reduces to one question: *Do you care enough to understand me?*

Every great communicator answers that question with their presence. They listen not to reply, not to manage, not to impress, but to honor.

Listening is love translated into attention.

It is how fathers heal children, how leaders rebuild trust, how communities rediscover compassion.

When you feel tempted to talk too much, remember:

"When you listen long enough, people start to hear themselves."

That's the moment when real transformation begins, not when you give answers, but when your silence allows another person's truth to surface.

Self-Reflection

1. When was the last time you truly listened without preparing a response?

2. Who in your life, at work or at home, might be waiting for you to hear what they haven't yet said aloud?

3. What might change if you treated silence not as awkwardness, but as reverence?

Habits that Matter

- **The Listening Ratio:** Aim to listen 70% of the time and speak 30% in your next conversation. Let silence fill the rest.

- **Mirror Practice:** When someone shares something meaningful, summarize it back in your own words: "What I'm hearing is...", not to prove attention, but to confirm care.

- **Pause Before Advice:** When tempted to fix or explain, ask, "Would you like me to listen or help?" You'll be surprised how often they say "Just listen."

- **The 24-Hour Rule:** When emotion runs high, delay major responses for one day. Listening improves with distance from defensiveness.

Speaking with Grace and Courage

There comes a moment in every leader's life, and every parent's, when silence is no longer kindness.

When the loving thing, the right thing, is to speak truth, even when your voice trembles.

I used to think grace and courage were opposites. Grace was softness, compassion, gentleness. Courage was firmness, conviction, the will to say what others would not. But over time I've learned that true leadership requires both, fused, not separated.

Grace without courage becomes sentimentality. Courage without grace becomes cruelty.

The art of communication lies in holding both at once, truth that heals, not harms; compassion that corrects, not enables.

This balance, this holy tension, is what is referred to as the language of leadership.

The Anatomy of a Hard Conversation

There's no escaping them. Whether you're leading an organization or raising a teenager, hard conversations are inevitable. The stakes are high because the relationship is high.

You can deliver a message perfectly structured, but if the spirit behind it is defensive or dismissive, it will fail. People rarely remember your phrasing, they remember how your words made them feel.

Over the years, I've developed a rhythm for difficult conversations that helps me stay grounded in both courage and grace:

1. **Begin with shared purpose:** Start by reaffirming the relationship, not the problem. "You matter to me, and I want us to find a way forward." This creates safety before challenge.

2. **Name reality with kindness:** Avoid vague language. Be clear about the issue, but choose words that describe behavior, not identity. "I noticed deadlines have slipped," not "You're unreliable."

3. **Invite perspective:** "Help me understand what's been happening from your side." Listening here is not a tactic, it's trust-building.

4. **Express belief in their capacity:** "I know you can do this," or "I've seen you handle tougher situations." Encouragement sustains accountability.

5. **End with partnership, not punishment:** "Let's work on this together." Ownership grows in shared soil, not imposed soil.

It sounds simple, but simplicity doesn't mean easy. Graceful truth-telling demands internal calm, empathy, and preparation. It requires doing your emotional homework before entering the room.

A hard conversation begins long before it's spoken, it begins in the quiet where you decide what your motive truly is: *to win, or to restore.*

The Courage to Be Clear
There's a tenderness in clarity.

We often avoid directness because we fear it will hurt. But vagueness wounds too, just slower, and deeper.

People deserve the dignity of clarity. It gives them direction and frees them from confusion.

I once worked alongside a young leader who struggled to give feedback. His team underperformed because he softened every critique into suggestion. "Maybe we could try..." or "Perhaps next time..." He meant well, but his hesitancy bred uncertainty.

One day, he was told, "You're not protecting them by being unclear, you're abandoning them."

He looked stunned. But over time, he realized that clarity, spoken with respect, is a form of care.

When I think of courage in communication, I don't picture shouting or dominance. I picture steady eyes, an honest tone, and a heart anchored in goodwill.

Courage is speaking truth in a way that allows others to still feel safe in your presence.

Words that Weigh and Words that Lift
There are two kinds of sentences in leadership: *those that weigh people down* and *those that lift them up.*

A weighted word limits. It begins with "you always" or "you never." It generalizes, accuses, and labels. These phrases bury people beneath your disappointment.

Lifting words, on the other hand, point to potential. They begin with, "I've noticed you're capable of..." or "I wonder if there's a better way we can..." They leave dignity intact.

I once had to address chronic lateness in a team member. I had tried reprimands, policy reminders, even humor, nothing worked.

Then I changed one line. Instead of saying, "You're always late," I began with, "When you're late, the team loses your energy, and that matters because you set the tone."

The behavior changed within weeks. Because the message shifted from criticism to contribution.

Our words either define people by their mistakes or remind them of their meaning. One destroys, the other redeems – one breathes life the other brings death.

Grace as Strength

Some mistake grace for weakness, as if kindness means avoiding confrontation. But grace is not the absence of truth; it's the manner in which truth is delivered.

Grace is strength under control. It's authority without arrogance.

When I was younger, I thought leadership required force. I raised my voice when I felt unheard. I equated volume with conviction. Over time, I learned that calm authority carries far more power than aggression.

Grace disarms defensiveness. It allows hard truths to land on soft soil.

I'll never forget a lesson from a senior leader I once worked with. After I'd made a costly error, I braced for a reprimand. Instead, he invited me to his office, closed the door, and said gently, "This mistake is serious, but I trust you'll learn from it. Let's figure out how and move forward."

That conversation shaped my entire leadership philosophy.
He didn't lower the standard, he lifted my capacity. That's what grace does.

The Father's Voice

Fatherhood, more than anything, taught me restraint.

There's a temptation, especially with children, to fill silence with correction, to lecture when listening would suffice. But the best lessons I've taught my kids were rarely in moments of discipline. They were in moments of quiet honesty.

Once, after my son made a poor choice at school, he came home expecting anger. Instead, I said, "I'm disappointed, but I believe in who you're becoming." He looked confused at first, then relieved, then thoughtful.

A week later, he told me, "I didn't want to let you down again."

That day, I understood that words spoken in grace don't remove accountability, they intensify it. Because love, when it's trusted, inspires responsibility.

In the workplace, the same principle holds true. People rise not when they're shamed into compliance, but when they're trusted into character.

The Power of Vulnerable Speech

Speaking courageously sometimes means admitting what you don't know.

There's immense trust built when a leader says, "I was wrong," or "I need your help." It's counterintuitive, we fear that vulnerability will undermine authority. But in truth, it deepens it.

I've watched teams rally around a leader who owned a mistake. I've seen families heal when a parent apologizes sincerely.

Vulnerability humanizes authority. It reminds people that leadership isn't perfection, it's authenticity in motion.

The most courageous sentence a leader can speak is often the simplest: "I'm sorry."

Because grace is not just what we extend to others; it's what we allow to move through us.

Speaking Peace into Storms

There's a line from Proverbs that says, *"A gentle answer turns away wrath, but a harsh word stirs up anger."*

Even without religion, the wisdom stands: tone dictates trajectory.

In moments of conflict, the way we speak determines whether the room burns hotter or cools into reason.

I've had meetings begin with tension so thick you could feel it in your chest. In those moments, I remind myself to lower my voice, slow my breathing, and choose words like cool water. Not to pacify, but to steady.

This is what mature communication does, it lowers the temperature without lowering the truth.

Self-Reflection

1. What difficult conversation are you avoiding right now, and what might it look like to approach it with both grace and courage?

2. When have your words brought calm to conflict, or heat to harmony?

3. How could vulnerability become part of your leadership voice this week?

Habits that Matter

- **Prepare, Don't Script:** Before hard conversations, write the key truth you must say, then rehearse tone, not words.

- **The Sandwich Principle (Redefined):** Instead of praise–critique–praise, use *connection–truth–commitment*. It builds trust without manipulation.

- **Apology Practice:** Once a week, notice an area (big or small) where you could say, "I'm sorry." Then do it, quickly, without justification.

- **Family Parallel:** Replace lectures with stories. When correction is needed, share a personal failure and what you learned. Grace through story heals faster than rules through reprimand.

The Language of Legacy

There are moments, often unremarkable at the time, when words become timeless.

A quiet conversation in a kitchen. A late-night phone call. A sentence said almost in passing. And years later, those same words resurface, guiding, comforting, anchoring.

That's the secret no one tells you about communication: it doesn't end when the conversation ends. Words outlive their moment. They echo through memory, shaping what others believe long after you've left the room, or this life.

We think legacy is written in achievements, but it's really carried in voices. The tone, the truth, the tenderness of how we spoke to people becomes our living echo.

The Echo Effect

Leadership is an echo chamber of the soul. What you say, and how you say it, reverberates through the culture you lead.

A careless remark from a manager can ripple through an entire department. A single moment of sincere praise can change someone's career. A compassionate word at the right time can outlast every spreadsheet and strategy you'll ever design.

Years ago, I led a project team under immense pressure. Tensions were high; deadlines tighter. One afternoon, after yet another setback, I gathered the team for what I thought would be a morale talk. I said, "We'll figure this out together. No one carries this alone."

I didn't think much of it, it was instinctive, said in the heat of leadership. But months later, one of the younger team members told me, "That sentence got me through the rest of the year."

It humbled me. It reminded me that the smallest words can create the loudest echoes, when spoken with sincerity.

The words we speak in leadership ripple outward; the words we speak in family ripple downward. Either way, they continue, shaping generations of culture, character, and courage.

What We Say When We Don't Speak

Silence speaks too, and often more loudly than words.

The absence of communication can become a message all its own: indifference, avoidance, pride, or peace.

A father who never says "I'm proud of you" teaches as much as one who says it often, just not the lesson he intends.

A leader who avoids conflict sends a message too, that truth is negotiable when comfort is at stake.

Our silence is part of our language. The question is whether it speaks neglect or wisdom.

Healthy silence invites reflection; harmful silence breeds distance.

As I grow older, I've learned that the legacy of my listening, the times I stayed present and patient, speaks just as loudly as the legacy of my words.

Presence becomes memory.
And memory becomes language in others.

The Stories People Tell

Every organization, like every family, eventually becomes a collection of stories. The stories told around the table, in the hallway, in the quiet moments after you've gone.

What stories will they tell about you?

Will they say, "She always made us feel heard"
"He spoke truth even when it was hard"
"He stayed calm when everyone else panicked"
"She believed in me before I did"

These are the true measures of communication, not eloquence or authority, but the emotional residue left behind.

In my years working with and in teams, I've found that the most beloved leaders are rarely remembered for their strategies. They're remembered for sentences:

- "I see potential in you."

- "You don't need to apologize for learning."

- "We'll figure this out together."

Their language becomes folklore, the living DNA of culture.

And in families, it's the same. Generations remember not what we taught, but how we spoke. They remember the tone, the laughter, the warmth. They remember how our words made them feel safe to become themselves.

That is legacy, trust carried in tone.

Words That Outlive the Speaker
My own father wasn't a man of many words, but he had a phrase he'd use often when things got hard. He'd say, "You can only take one step at a time."

It used to frustrate me, simple, almost cliché. But now, in seasons of chaos or grief, those words return like a calm tide. They're no longer his; they've become mine.

Every time I say them, to my kids, my colleagues, myself, I hear his voice folded inside mine. That's legacy. It's the continuation of care across time.

Leaders, like fathers, must remember this: your words today are someone's inner dialogue tomorrow. The tone you use in correction will become the tone they use in self-reflection. The encouragement you give will become courage in their decisions.

We are always, in some way, teaching people how to talk to themselves.

That's why speech is sacred, it's inheritance in motion.

Repairing the Echo
Of course, not every word we've spoken has been wise. We've all said things we regret, in anger, in fatigue, in fear.

But legacy is not perfection; it's repair.

I once apologized to a team for a harsh comment I'd made during a stressful project. It was uncomfortable, the room was quiet, no one quite knew what to say. Then one team member nodded and said, "That means a lot. We've all been there."

The tension broke. Trust returned.

In families, the same rule holds. A heartfelt apology, "I shouldn't have said that", can rewrite years of distance. Children remember humility more than they remember perfection.

Repair is how we edit our legacy while we're still here to hold the pen.

The Language of Blessing
In ancient cultures, blessings were spoken aloud, deliberate, poetic words bestowed by elders to affirm identity and destiny.

Somewhere along the way, we lost that practice. But I think we need it back, in boardrooms and in homes.

To bless someone is to name the good you see in them, to speak future into their present. It costs nothing, yet it's one of the rarest forms of communication in leadership today.

When you tell someone, "You have a gift for bringing calm," or "Your integrity anchors this team," you're not flattering them, you're fortifying them.

Blessing is the most powerful leadership tool I know. It builds cultures of gratitude instead of comparison, growth instead of insecurity.

And at home, it's the same. I've started telling my children the traits I see emerging in them, not just achievements, but essence. "You're becoming brave," "You're a good listener," "You have a kind strength."

Their posture changes instantly, not from pride, but from peace. Words of blessing teach them who they are before the world tries to tell them otherwise.

That is legacy in its purest form: language that carries identity forward.

The Voice That Remains

Someday, our meetings will end. Our desks will be cleared. Our names will fade from organizational charts.

But our words will remain, in the cadence of conversations, in the way people comfort one another, in the quiet voices that carry our tone long after we've gone.

When people talk about us, and they will, they'll remember how we made them feel.

Did our words build courage or fear?
Did our tone create calm or anxiety?
Did our silence nurture or neglect?

Those are the questions worth living with.

The leaders and fathers who understand this speak as if every word is a brick in someone else's foundation. They measure not by eloquence, but by endurance.

Because the greatest communicators don't just move audiences, they move hearts into alignment with truth.

Self-Reflection

1. What sentence or phrase from someone in your past still shapes how you see yourself today?

2. What do you hope others will remember about the way you spoke to them, your tone, your truth, your grace?

3. Where might your silence be sending the wrong message, and how could you speak life instead?

Habits that Matter

- **Legacy Journal:** Write down three sentences you want your team or children to remember you by. Start living them out this week.

- **Repair in Real Time:** If you notice you've spoken harshly, apologize within 24 hours. Immediate repair strengthens trust's foundation.

- **Blessing Habit:** Once a week, intentionally affirm someone's unique contribution, not for results, but for character.

- **Echo Awareness:** Record yourself during a meeting or conversation and listen back. Does your tone sound like the leader, or the father, you want to be remembered as?

Closing Thought

In the end, all leadership becomes language. And all language becomes legacy.

The titles fade, the projects finish, the applause quiets, but the words we've spoken remain.

To lead like a father is to understand that every word has a lifespan far longer than our own and Communication strengthens the FatherFrame™ by turning presence and priorities into connection, trust, and shared meaning.

It's to speak with awareness that our tone today becomes someone's strength tomorrow.

The language of trust is not built in speeches; it's built in sentences.

The language of legacy is not written in stone; it's written in hearts.

Let that echo be kind. Let it be true. Let it be love, spoken aloud.

Clear communication sets direction, but without discipline it drifts into aspiration. After all, words create expectation, but habits create reality.

The next chapter leads us into discipline, not as rigidity or perfectionism, but as the quiet strength of consistency. It is here that leadership begins to take shape in the ordinary, repeatable acts that form the atmosphere people come to rely on.

Chapter Four – Discipline: The Strength of Consistency

"Consistency is the invisible force that stabilizes families and teams, small, repeated actions done well build trust faster than intensity ever will."

Consistency is the currency of credibility. In homes and workplaces alike, people anchor themselves to what you repeatedly do, not what you occasionally say.

This chapter explores how small, disciplined habits compound into trust, stability, and long-term performance. Rather than presenting discipline as rigidity, it reframes it as reliability: the steady, predictable presence that gives others confidence to move, grow, and take risks. When leaders practice discipline in the small things, the big things take care of themselves.

Discipline is a quiet pillar of the FatherFrame™, not the harsh kind, but the steady consistency that builds reliability over time. It is the strength that makes presence sustainable and communication believable.

The Rhythm of Reliability

Discipline has become a misunderstood word. For many, it conjures images of restriction, rigidity, even punishment. But in its truest form, discipline isn't about control, it's about *commitment*.

It's the steady heartbeat beneath every act of integrity. It's what remains when the excitement fades, when the applause stops, when no one else is watching.

Discipline is a quiet pillar of the FatherFrame™, not the harsh kind, but the steady consistency that builds reliability over time. It is the strength that makes presence sustainable and communication believable.

Leadership and fatherhood share this same truth: the people who depend on you don't need your perfection, they need your predictability.

Reliability is love in rhythm.

The Comfort of Consistency

When my children were young, bedtime was sacred. The routine never changed: a story, a prayer, the bedtime train. Some nights I was tired, other nights distracted, but I learned early that the ritual mattered more than my mood.

One evening, running late after a long day, I tried to skip the story. My daughter, half-asleep, whispered, "But you always read."

Her words landed softly but deeply. That's when I realized: consistency isn't about routine for its own sake, it's about safety. Predictability tells people, *You can trust me to show up.*

In leadership, it's the same. Teams don't thrive on charisma; they thrive on consistency.

They don't need fireworks; they need foundations.

I was about to take over a new team, a team that had been underperforming and had experienced a number of internal staff complaints. I was talking to one of the team members, and she had told me that they were looking forward to me coming on board. I jokingly said "Be careful what you wish for, you may hate me". And she replied "Just be consistent – that's all we want".

Reliability builds psychological safety, the invisible assurance that says, "This person means what they say."

A consistent leader doesn't need to raise their voice to be respected. Their steadiness speaks louder than any command.

Reliability as Leadership's Hidden Currency
In a world obsessed with innovation and disruption, reliability sounds almost unfashionable. But it's the trait every great leader is built upon.

The best organizations I've seen are not those that constantly reinvent, but those that execute the basics with relentless excellence. They show up, every day, in the same direction.

Reliability is the quiet currency of trust.

When people know what to expect from you, they can focus on what matters, not managing your moods or guessing your standards.

I once worked as a senior executive within a team that was high-performing but perpetually anxious. Turnover was climbing, morale slipping. When I attended the meetings, the reason became clear: the Leader was unpredictable. Brilliant one day, abrupt the next. His inconsistency created constant emotional recalibration for those around him.

He didn't need to change his strategy, he needed to stabilize his *spirit*.

After months of reflection and coaching, he began to slow down, respond instead of react, and build rituals into his leadership, weekly check-ins, consistent tone, predictable follow-up. Within six months, his team's engagement scores rose by 30%.

Consistency had done what charisma never could, it created calm.

The Father's Mirror
Fathers, too, shape worlds through rhythm.

Children measure the world not in words, but in patterns, the rhythm of your steps, the tone of your voice, the way the morning unfolds.

When life feels uncertain, it's consistency that anchors them.

My son once asked, "Dad, are you coming to my game this weekend?" I said yes, but work ran long, and I missed it. That night, I tried to explain, traffic, meetings, deadlines, but his eyes told me what words couldn't fix.

He didn't need my excuses; he needed my example.

Reliability is love's most practical form. It's showing up when it's inconvenient, following through when it's unnoticed, staying steady when it's hard.

In that sense, discipline is not control, it's *care expressed through consistency*.

When Routine Becomes Rhythm

Discipline begins with routine, but it matures into rhythm. Routine is mechanical, the checklist of duties. Rhythm is relational, it's the harmony of purpose and pattern.

You can feel the difference. Routine drains; rhythm sustains. Routine says "I have to." Rhythm says "I get to."

A father who reads a bedtime story out of obligation performs a task. A father who reads because he loves the closeness creates ritual.

A leader who holds Monday meetings because "that's what we do" fills time. A leader who uses them to listen, encourage, and refocus sets tempo.

When discipline becomes rhythm, it turns from repetition into relationship.

The same pattern plays out in teams. When people know the rhythm of your leadership, when they can trust that the same standards, the same fairness, the same calmness will meet them every day, they relax. Creativity grows in predictability, not chaos.

Rhythm doesn't stifle freedom; it enables it.

The Neuroscience of Predictability

The brain, fascinatingly, craves consistency.

Neuroscientists have shown that predictable environments reduce cortisol levels and boost dopamine, the brain's reward chemical. In other words, stability literally makes people calmer and more motivated.

This is why children thrive with structure, and why teams thrive with clarity.

Uncertainty keeps the body in low-grade stress, the kind that doesn't scream, but quietly erodes confidence and creativity.

When a leader's behavior is steady, the team's nervous system settles.
When a parent's tone is stable, the child's brain feels safe.

That's why discipline, showing up consistently, is one of the most compassionate things we can do for others. It tells their bodies, "You can rest now. You know what to expect."

The Slow Beauty of Repetition
Modern culture worships novelty, but mastery belongs to repetition.

The musician practicing scales.
The athlete training drills.
The father packing lunches.
The leader reviewing the same daily metrics.

Repetition refines character. It teaches humility, patience, and precision.

There's a Japanese phrase, *kaizen*, meaning "continuous improvement." It's not about dramatic leaps, but small, consistent steps. The art of doing something slightly better today than yesterday.

That's the heart of discipline: slow faithfulness.

When my children were little, I'd tuck them in the same way every night. The same song, the same prayer. I wondered sometimes if it mattered. But now that they're grown, they remember every word.

Discipline builds memory, not just for you, but for others. The repetition of care becomes the rhythm of their belonging.

When Consistency Becomes Character

The most disciplined people aren't rigid, they're reliable. They've aligned their habits with their values so deeply that integrity becomes instinct.

They don't wake up deciding whether to do the right thing; they've already built a rhythm that does it for them.

That's why small disciplines matter so much, not because they impress others, but because they train your spirit to stay aligned when the spotlight's gone.

As the philosopher Will Durant once wrote, *"We are what we repeatedly do. Excellence, then, is not an act but a habit."*

Consistency is how values survive chaos.

Self-Reflection

1. Where in your life are you dependable, and where are you drifting into inconsistency?

2. What small rituals bring stability to your family or team?

3. When people describe your leadership, do they use words like "steady," "predictable," or "grounded"? If not, what needs to change?

Habits that Matter

- **Reliability Audit:** Ask three people close to you, one at work, one at home, one friend, "Can you count on me to follow through?" Listen humbly to their answer.

- **Anchor Ritual:** Create one daily or weekly rhythm that grounds you (a walk, a prayer, a reflection). Protect it fiercely.

- **Tone Tracker:** Choose a consistent emotional tone to bring into meetings or family meals, calm, optimistic, attentive, and hold it for a week.

- **Show Up Anyway:** Pick one task this week that feels inconvenient but important. Do it simply because you said you would.

The Discipline of Small Things

Greatness rarely announces itself. It doesn't arrive with fanfare or lightning bolts. It slips quietly into ordinary routines, in the way we begin our mornings, handle interruptions, keep promises, and close our days.

In leadership and in fatherhood, it is the small things, the details we're tempted to overlook, that form the architecture of trust.

The myth of transformation is that it's grand. The truth of transformation is that it's *gradual*.

Discipline begins in the hidden corners: the small, repeated actions that seem trivial in isolation but compound into character over time.

The Hidden Weight of Small Habits

When my children were little, I kept a ritual that seemed almost absurdly simple. Every morning, before they left for school, I would look them in the eyes and say, "I love you. Be kind. Be brave."

It took less than ten seconds. But I never skipped it, no matter how late, no matter how distracted.

Years later, one of my daughters told me that those three words, *kind* and *brave*, became her compass. Whenever she faced a hard moment, she'd pause and think, *What would Dad say right now?*

That's when I understood: the smallest habits can hold the heaviest meaning.

Leaders often chase the dramatic gesture, the big speech, the major initiative, but people are shaped by what you do consistently, not occasionally.

Micro-integrity matters. Keeping your word on little things teaches people they can trust you with big ones. Answering an email when you said you would, showing up on time, saying "thank you" every day, these aren't etiquette; they're evidence.

How you do anything, is how you do everything. Every act of reliability, no matter how small, deposits trust in the relational bank account. And those deposits sustain you when inevitable withdrawals come.

Micro-Integrity: Doing the Right Thing When No One Notices
Integrity isn't a single decision, it's a thousand small ones, repeated when no one is keeping score.

It's logging the correct hours on your timesheet even when you could round up.

It's giving credit to a colleague who helped you, even if their contribution was quiet.

It's admitting you were wrong without waiting to be caught.

These moments don't trend on social media, but they build moral muscle.

I once worked with a warehouse manager named Luke. He wasn't flashy or loud. He rarely spoke in meetings. But everyone trusted him implicitly. Why? Because he was relentlessly consistent in the small things. He stacked boxes neatly. He swept the floor after every shift. He remembered birthdays.

His influence was quiet, but undeniable. When leadership positions opened, his name always came up first. He never had to self-promote; his habits had already spoken for him.

Micro-integrity is invisible leadership. It's what happens when no one is watching, but everyone feels its effects.

The Neuroscience of Tiny Wins
Behavioral psychology calls this the "compound effect", small, repeated actions that accumulate into exponential results.

James Clear, in *Atomic Habits*, explains that if you improve by just 1% every day, you'll be 37 times better by year's end. The math may be theoretical, but the principle is ancient: *faithfulness in little things builds capacity for greater things*.

Neuroscience backs this up. Every time you complete a small, consistent task, making the bed, following through on a promise, ending your day with reflection, your brain releases a small hit of dopamine, reinforcing a sense of progress and control.

Over time, those micro-rewards hardwire the identity of a disciplined person.

That's why small things matter so much. They're not just tasks; they're signals to your brain about who you are.

U.S. Navy Admiral William H. McRaven argued in his 2014 speech that went viral, that if you cannot do the little things right like simply making your bed in the morning, you will never be able to do the big things right.

A person who keeps small promises believes in their own reliability.

A leader who maintains simple rituals teaches the brain that structure is safety.

A family that shares small daily habits learns that love is consistency made visible.

The Paradox of the Ordinary

We tend to romanticize breakthroughs, those defining moments when everything changes. But breakthroughs rarely happen without the grind that preceded them.

Excellence, in any domain, is built on the boring.

The world's best athletes train on fundamentals. The most enduring organizations refine their processes endlessly. The healthiest families run on ordinary routines, meals, chores, bedtime rituals, that look mundane but form deep emotional glue.

I once visited a CEO known for his visionary style. But when I shadowed him for a day, I discovered his true gift wasn't inspiration, it was *discipline of detail*.

He reviewed the same weekly report every Friday without fail. He wrote handwritten thank-you notes to staff anniversaries. He started every meeting exactly on time, every single time.

None of it was glamorous. But it created a culture where people felt anchored.

When crisis hit, that foundation of consistency became their stability.

The extraordinary, it turns out, is just the ordinary done faithfully.

Fatherhood and the Art of Small Gestures

Fatherhood, too, is built on small things done with big love.

It's the way you tie a shoe slowly when you're running late. The way you listen to a half-made-up story with full attention. The way you remember a favorite snack after a tough day.

None of it will appear in a biography, but all of it lives in memory.

One evening, after I'd had a hard day at work, I came home tired and distracted. My youngest daughter was sitting at the table coloring. As I passed by, she looked up and said, "I saved a crayon for you."

I sat down. We colored together for ten minutes in silence.

That night, I realized that small moments aren't interruptions to life; they *are* life. The same applies in leadership, the passing hallway chat, the quick thank-you email, the genuine "how are you?" between meetings. Those are the moments people remember.

Consistency in small kindnesses becomes the culture people trust.

When the Small Things Slip
We all drift. The small disciplines that once grounded us begin to erode under the weight of busyness.

We skip the check-ins. We rush the greetings. We stop saying "please" and "thank you."

No single moment breaks trust, it's the slow fade of attention that does.

That's why self-awareness is the first act of discipline. You can't maintain small consistencies if you've stopped noticing them.

When I feel that drift, when I catch myself becoming careless with tone, punctuality, or presence, I go back to basics.
I ask:

- Did I keep my word today?

- Did I show up with attention, not just attendance?

- Did I do the small things that signal respect?

The answer isn't always yes. But asking the question is its own discipline, it resets the rhythm before dissonance grows.

From Habit to Honor

When you commit to small disciplines, something beautiful happens: your habits start to honor others.

A leader who arrives early communicates, *Your time matters.*
A father who listens without his phone says, *Your story matters.*
A colleague who follows through says, *Our shared work matters.*

Discipline becomes devotion. Routine becomes reverence.

The greatest leaders I've known had this quiet honor about them, a dignity in detail. They didn't chase applause; they chased alignment. Every small act was an expression of who they were becoming.

That's what discipline really is, the art of becoming trustworthy, one choice at a time.

Self-Reflection

1. What "small things" in your daily routine might carry hidden weight for those around you?

2. Which neglected habits, if revived, would immediately improve the trust others place in you?

3. How could you make your ordinary routines expressions of love rather than obligation?

Habits that Matter

- **The One-Minute Habit:** Choose one simple, repeatable action that takes less than a minute (like sending a thank-you text or making your bed). Do it every day for a month. Notice the ripple.

- **Micro-Integrity Tracker:** For one week, note each time you keep a small promise. If you break one, note it too, not for guilt, but for awareness.

- **Repetition Ritual:** Identify a small family or team ritual (morning check-in, end-of-day gratitude, Friday recap). Make it sacred.

- **Slow the Small Moments:** When tempted to rush through something routine, pause for 30 seconds and do it with full attention.

Leading Through Routine

Leadership, like parenthood, is far less about grand moments than it is about rhythm. Most of our lives are lived in repetition, the daily return to meetings, meals, decisions, commutes, and conversations. It's within those repetitions that culture is shaped and character is revealed.

The modern world glorifies spontaneity and innovation, but the truth is that *routine is the scaffolding that holds everything creative, meaningful, and enduring in place.* Great leaders, and great parents, understand that the strength of a system lies not in its occasional brilliance, but in its daily faithfulness.

The Architecture of Rhythm

A few years ago, I was working for a social enterprise that struggled with inconsistency. Every week, the focus shifted, one day a new marketing campaign, the next a rebranding exercise, then an urgent shift in reporting. The team was talented but exhausted.

When we asked what rhythm anchored their week, they laughed nervously. "Every week's different," one said.

So, we built something simple: a weekly rhythm. Mondays for planning, Wednesdays for team check-ins, Fridays for gratitude and reflection. Within two months, tension dropped, creativity rose, and burnout declined.

Nothing else changed, same people, same workload. But now their energy had a cadence. Predictability became peace.

That's the paradox of routine: far from constraining us, it liberates our energy for what matters most.

In family life, rhythm plays the same role. Children flourish when they know the tempo of their days. Morning routines, family dinners, weekend chores, these aren't just logistics; they're love in pattern form. They whisper, *You belong. You're safe here.*

The best homes, like the best teams, hum with a quiet, consistent rhythm, a pulse that steadies everyone within it.

The Myth of the Mundane

Routine has a bad reputation. We associate it with boredom, monotony, even mediocrity. But that's only when it becomes mindless.

Mindful routine, on the other hand, is one of the most powerful tools for sustaining energy and excellence.

When I was leading a large division, I had a morning ritual: a coffee at the same desk, five minutes of stillness, then my "three questions" journal.

1. Who needs encouragement today?

2. What deserves gratitude?

3. What must not be left undone?

It took less than ten minutes, but it transformed my days. It aligned my leadership with intention rather than reaction.

People often ask how I stayed calm under pressure. The answer isn't glamorous, I simply refused to start the day in chaos. Routine became resistance against the tyranny of urgency.

The same principle works in families. A consistent morning or evening rhythm, even something as simple as breakfast together or walking the dog at sunset, builds more resilience than any motivational speech ever could.

Because routine isn't the opposite of passion; it's what keeps passion from burning out.

The Neuroscience of Rhythm and Energy

Our bodies crave rhythm because our brains run on it. Circadian rhythms, hormonal cycles, and neural pathways all depend on predictable patterns. Disruption creates stress; repetition creates stability.

Studies show that people who maintain daily routines experience lower levels of anxiety and higher productivity. The reason is simple: predictability frees cognitive energy. When the brain doesn't have to decide when to wake, eat, or focus, it can devote more energy to creativity and problem-solving.

For the same reason, Mark Zuckerberg decided in his early career to wear the same jeans and t-shirt everyday. Removing the decision on what to wear today from his morning, freed up his mind and energy to concentrate on growing Facebook.

For leaders, this insight is gold. Establishing structured rhythms, standing meetings, fixed review days, consistent communication formats, reduces decision fatigue and stabilizes team energy.

In parenting, routine does the same thing emotionally. Children don't need constant excitement; they need steady presence. Repetition becomes reassurance.

That's why bedtime rituals are so powerful, they literally regulate a child's nervous system. The cadence of familiar actions, story, hug, light off, signals safety and belonging.

Rhythm, then, is not restriction. It's neuroscience in service of peace.

Leadership as a Daily Liturgy

I often think of leadership routines as a kind of *liturgy*, sacred repetitions that shape who we become.

The ancient monastic communities understood this. Their days were structured around fixed hours of prayer, work, and rest, not because they feared chaos, but because they knew consistency invites clarity. They built rhythm to keep their souls aligned with their purpose.

Modern leadership needs the same philosophy. Our calendars may look different, but the intent is the same: to create space for meaning within motion.

One CEO I admire begins every executive meeting with one question: "Who did we serve this week, and how did it feel?" It's become ritual. And that ritual reminds the organization that numbers exist to serve people, not the other way around.

In family life, we too can create liturgies, small, sacred habits that orient the soul. A shared meal, a Sunday walk, a nightly word of blessing. These practices don't just manage time; they teach values through repetition.

A father's consistency becomes a moral compass. A leader's routine becomes a company's conscience.

Recovering Meaning in Repetition
The challenge of routine is that it can slip into autopilot. When it does, we lose the meaning behind the movement. That's why discipline must be paired with mindfulness, awareness that transforms repetition into ritual.

I once led a weekly briefing that had grown dull. People came late, half-listened, and left uninspired. The content was fine; the spirit was gone.

So one morning, I opened differently: "Before we start, tell me one thing, one outcome you're proud of this week."

It took five minutes. But that small shift reignited energy. The meeting felt purposeful again.

Routine without reflection becomes rote.
Routine with reflection becomes renewal.

The same applies at home. When bedtime stories start to feel like chores, or dinner conversations become transactional, pause and remind yourself: *this moment is shaping memory*. That awareness turns ordinary rituals into holy ground.

My former father-in-law would always say "making memories"

Great leaders and fathers don't escape routine, they *infuse it with intention*.

When Life Disrupts the Rhythm
Even the best rhythms get disrupted, illness, crisis, loss, transition. In those seasons, discipline shows its true strength: it becomes the muscle memory of hope.

When everything else collapses, the smallest rituals, a morning coffee, a journal entry, a shared prayer, remind you who you are.

I've lived this truth. During one of the hardest seasons of my career, when the pressure was unbearable and every day felt uncertain, I clung to one habit: writing down three good things before bed. Some nights I could only list one: *I'm still here.*

But over time, that discipline became a lifeline. Routine gave shape to resilience.

Families, too, find strength in rhythm during hardship. When loss or fear enters the home, maintaining even one small routine, a meal, a bedtime story, a walk, whispers, *We may be hurting, but we're still whole.*

Self-Reflection

1. Which parts of your day or week carry unintentional chaos that could be steadied by rhythm?

2. What daily routines, at work or home, already sustain your energy, and how could you protect them more deliberately?

3. Where have you lost meaning in your repetitions, and what small adjustment could reignite purpose?

Habits that Matter

- **Morning Anchor:** Choose one consistent morning ritual that grounds you, journaling, meditation, or a quiet walk. Do it before checking any device.

- **Rhythm Audit:** Map your week. Identify one area where inconsistency drains energy (e.g., communication, sleep, meetings). Create a simple recurring rhythm for it.

- **Micro-Liturgy:** Add one "meaning ritual" to an existing routine, like gratitude before meetings or affirmation before school.

- **Rhythm Reset:** If life feels chaotic, simplify. Drop one optional commitment and reinforce one core routine that truly matters.

The Cost and Gift of Consistency

Consistency is one of the most misunderstood virtues in leadership and in life.

From the outside, it looks effortless, calm, reliable, unwavering. But those who live it know the truth: consistency always costs something. It costs comfort. It costs novelty. It costs the constant craving for recognition.

To be consistent in character, in values, in compassion, when the world around you is reactive and impulsive, is an act of quiet rebellion.

Consistency doesn't dazzle. It doesn't draw applause. Yet, it is the bedrock upon which trust is built and legacies are sustained.

The world is full of talent and passion, but it bends toward those who simply keep showing up.

The Weight of Staying the Course

I remember sitting across from a young executive once who confessed, "I'm tired of being steady. Everyone else gets to pivot, try new things, take risks. I'm just... dependable."

He said it like it was a curse.

But dependability is not dullness. It's depth. It's the discipline of aligning yourself with purpose, even when it's inconvenient.

Consistency means *saying yes again* to what matters most, even when it no longer feels exciting.

That's the unseen emotional weight of leadership: the strength to remain anchored when enthusiasm fades.

In families, this same weight exists, the repetitive duties that no one applauds: making breakfast, folding laundry, paying bills, listening again to a story you've heard a dozen times.

You do it not because it's thrilling, but because love has rhythm, and its beat is often mundane.

The most heroic acts of care are rarely spontaneous; they're consistent.

The Ethical Weight of Dependability
There's a moral dimension to consistency.
It's not just about discipline, it's about dignity.

People have a right to count on your word, your tone, your integrity.

I once worked with a CEO who said, "I'd rather someone be consistently average than unpredictably brilliant." He wasn't celebrating mediocrity, he was naming the ethical power of reliability.

Inconsistent leaders erode trust, even when their intentions are good.
Because what people crave most is not brilliance, it's safety.

Consistency communicates safety. It says, *you won't be blindsided by my moods or motives.*

It's an ethical contract, a promise that your inner life won't spill harmfully into the lives of those you lead or love.

That's why the discipline of self-management is not selfishness; it's service. The calmer you are inside, the safer others feel around you.

Consistency, then, is leadership's moral backbone, not because it's glamorous, but because it's *good.*

The Cost of Steadiness in a Fickle World

Modern culture doesn't reward steadiness; it rewards novelty.

We celebrate the disruptor, the changer, the one who reinvents constantly. And yet, for every visionary breakthrough, there are hundreds of unsung individuals quietly keeping things running.

The irony is that every revolution still depends on someone consistent enough to execute it.

The cost of consistency is invisibility. You will rarely be thanked for being stable.

The meeting that went smoothly because you prepared.
The crisis that never happened because you anticipated it.
The relationship that stayed whole because you listened instead of reacted.

No one celebrates what didn't fall apart.

But that's what consistency does, it prevents chaos before it's visible.

I once asked a colleague why she never seemed rattled. She said, "I made peace with not needing to be noticed. My reward is knowing I didn't add to the noise."

That's the quiet nobility of consistency: it's invisible success.

When Consistency Feels Like a Burden

There are seasons when the call to stay steady feels heavy, when commitment begins to taste like confinement.

Every disciplined person faces this tension: the ache between responsibility and restlessness.

In my own life, I've felt it many times, especially as a father and leader. There are days you want to escape the weight of dependability, to be reckless, spontaneous, carefree. But then you remember that steadiness is someone's security.

Consistency is costly because it's relational. You don't do it for yourself; you do it for the ones counting on you.

But here's the paradox, the very thing that feels restrictive eventually becomes freeing.

Because when your actions align with your values, your soul finds peace. You no longer wrestle with guilt or self-doubt. You know who you are and what you stand for.

That's the gift buried inside the cost.

The Gift Hidden in Repetition
When you commit to doing something consistently, leading with fairness, showing up on time, holding your word, you start to notice something subtle: it gets easier.

What was once effort becomes instinct. The discipline that felt heavy turns graceful.

There's a rhythm of peace that emerges when your habits and your identity harmonize.

This is what the Stoic philosophers called *eudaimonia*, the state of flourishing that comes from living in accordance with one's values.

In spiritual terms, it's the grace of habit. In corporate terms, it's sustainable excellence.

I've seen this grace in seasoned leaders who've led through decades of change. Their steadiness isn't mechanical; it's soulful.

They've learned to see consistency not as confinement but as craft, like a musician repeating scales until they disappear into melody.

They no longer need to *try* to be consistent, they *are* consistency, embodied.

That's mastery.

Consistency as the Language of Trust
Trust is earned in moments, but built through consistency.

Think of the people you trust most. It's rarely because they made a single grand gesture. It's because they kept showing up, day after day, word after word, year after year.

Trust is the cumulative effect of predictability.

When a leader says, "I'll handle it," and they do, trust compounds.

When a father promises, "I'll be there," and he is, love compounds.

Broken trust, on the other hand, isn't shattered by catastrophe; it's eroded by inconsistency.

That's why the most powerful sentence in leadership may be: *"You can count on me."*

Not because it's poetic, but because it's rare.

Turning Monotony into Mastery
There's a danger in equating consistency with stagnation. But the truth is, mastery lives inside monotony.

When you do something repeatedly, whether it's writing, teaching, parenting, or leading, you begin to refine subtleties no one else can see. You notice patterns, anticipate problems, move with intuition instead of reaction.

The mundane becomes musical.

Michelangelo once said, *"If people knew how hard I had to work to gain my mastery, it would not seem so wonderful at all."*
The wonder was built through repetition.

In his prime, Usain Bolt trained 6 days a week, 11months of the year. Went to the gym for 90 minutes everyday to improve his endurance, speed and agility – all to run 100 and 200 meters at the Olympic Games every four years.

Leadership works the same way. The more consistently you practice fairness, communication, and calm under pressure, the more naturally excellence flows.

Routine turns into artistry when it's done with awareness.

The Grace of Unfinished Work
Consistency also teaches humility, the acceptance that progress is incremental and unfinished.

You don't have to get everything right today; you just have to stay in rhythm.

Like a father who keeps showing up even when the conversation is hard, or a leader who keeps holding standards even when morale dips, consistency says, *We're not there yet, but we're still moving.*

That humility guards against burnout. Because you stop demanding perfection and start honoring perseverance.

Self-Reflection

1. Where are you being called to stay steady, even though no one notices?

2. What part of your leadership or parenting feels monotonous, and how might you see it instead as practice toward mastery?

3. Who in your world needs to know they can count on you again, not through words, but through consistency?

Habits that Matter

- **Invisible Wins Journal:** Each night, write one quiet act of consistency you upheld today. Honor it, even if no one else saw.

- **Trust Ledger:** List five people who rely on your steadiness. Next to each name, note one small action that would reinforce their trust this week.

- **Mindful Repetition:** Choose a repetitive task (emailing, cooking, driving). Do it slowly, with gratitude, noticing its rhythm.

- **Consistency Covenant:** Identify one area where inconsistency has crept in (timeliness, tone, promises). Set a 30-day goal to restore alignment.

The Long Obedience: Endurance and Grace

There's a phrase that has guided my life through both leadership and fatherhood, *"A long obedience in the same direction."*

It comes from theologian Eugene Peterson to describe the quiet heroism of faithfulness. It's the kind of life that refuses to chase every distraction, that chooses to keep showing up when novelty fades and applause dies out.

In a world addicted to immediacy, endurance feels countercultural.

But the truth is, nothing lasting, no marriage, no organization, no legacy, is built without it.

Endurance is love stretched over time.

It is discipline carried to its fullest form, not perfection, but persistence, rooted in grace.

The Beauty of the Long Road

When you've led or parented for long enough, you start to see that the real victories aren't in the dramatic moments. They're in the long, slow arc of faithfulness.

You look back over years of choices, the meetings you didn't cancel, the apologies you made, the habits you kept, and you realize: endurance built this.

I once listened to a founder who had led his organization for twenty-five years. When asked what was the secret to longevity, he smiled and said, "I just kept showing up when I didn't feel like it."

There was no magic. Just endurance, humble, unspectacular, steady.

Fatherhood mirrors that same truth. It's not the grand vacations or the surprise gestures that define a relationship. It's the small, everyday repetitions: breakfast together, showing up to the game, saying goodnight even when you're tired.

Over decades, those small consistencies stack into love that lasts.

Fatigue as a Teacher
No one endures without encountering fatigue.

Every leader, every parent, every disciplined soul hits seasons where the weight of showing up feels too heavy to carry.

The temptation in those moments is to interpret tiredness as failure, to think, *If I were stronger, I wouldn't feel this way.* But fatigue is not failure; it's feedback. It tells us we are finite, human, in need of rest.

Endurance without grace becomes exhaustion.

When I burned out early in my career, it wasn't because I lacked stamina. It was because I confused endurance with self-neglect. I believed leadership meant never stopping, never showing weakness.

Grace corrected that lie. Grace reminded me that rest is not retreat; it's replenishment.

Now, I teach my teams, and my children, that strength is not measured by how long you can go without stopping, but by how wisely you know when to.

The long obedience isn't about endless motion; it's about faithful rhythm, effort and exhale, push and pause.

Endurance as a Spiritual Discipline

There's something sacred about choosing to stay the course when emotion and motivation have run dry. It's an act of quiet faith, a belief that what you're building matters, even when you can't see the outcome.

In the spiritual sense, endurance is worship through persistence. In the practical sense, it's leadership through alignment.

A father keeps guiding, even when his children seem distant.
A leader keeps leading, even when the results are slow.
A team keeps striving, even when recognition is delayed.

That's endurance, doing what's right, not because it's rewarding, but because it's *true*.

It's a posture of integrity that whispers: *I will stay, because staying itself is sacred.*

And grace is what sustains that posture. Grace is what reminds you that you are not the sum of your productivity, that your worth doesn't depend on performance.

Discipline gets you started. Endurance keeps you going. Grace carries you home.

The Seasons of Discipline

Discipline isn't static; it has seasons.

In your twenties, it looks like ambition, long hours, relentless drive.

In your forties, it becomes endurance, sustaining focus, navigating fatigue.

And later in life, it matures into wisdom, knowing what to hold and what to release.

The secret is learning to adjust your pace as your seasons change.

What served you in one stage may break you in another.

I watched my father approach retirement. He confessed, "I don't know how to stop driving so hard. I've been in motion my whole life."

I told him, "Discipline isn't just about doing, it's about *being aligned.* Sometimes the most disciplined thing you can do is rest."

He nodded quietly. Months later, he wrote to me, saying, "I'm learning to be faithful to stillness."

That's the beauty of endurance, it evolves. It becomes gentler, slower, deeper. It's no longer about holding everything together; it's about holding only what matters.

Grace: The Finishing Power
Grace doesn't oppose discipline; it perfects it.

Where discipline builds structure, grace fills it with spirit. Where consistency maintains effort, grace gives it meaning.

Without grace, discipline becomes drudgery, a treadmill of obligation. With grace, discipline becomes devotion, an offering of love.

Grace allows you to forgive yourself when you falter, to begin again without shame.
It turns the "must" of duty into the "may" of purpose.

I remember once missing a family dinner for work. I'd promised to be there, but a crisis pulled me away. When I got home, my daughter said, "It's okay, Dad. I know you wanted to be here."

Her words were pure grace, unearned, undeserved. But they didn't excuse my failure; they inspired my recommitment.

That's how grace works. It doesn't let you off the hook, it strengthens your hands to hold the line again.

Grace, not guilt, is what sustains long-term discipline.

The Inheritance of Endurance

The fruit of endurance isn't immediate. It ripens over years, sometimes decades.

When people look back on your leadership, or your fatherhood, they won't remember the busy seasons or the accolades. They'll remember your *presence over time*.

They'll say, "He was steady."
"She stayed kind."
"They didn't quit when it got hard."

That's the inheritance endurance leaves behind, the quiet assurance that love can be trusted to last.

When you've lived long enough in rhythm, those who come after you inherit not just your results, but your resilience. They'll draw strength from the story of your staying.

Endurance as Love Made Visible

Endurance is love's most convincing evidence.

Because love that lasts is not the product of feeling, it's the fruit of faithfulness.

Every act of endurance, every time you show up again, forgive again, lead again, becomes an unspoken sermon.

The people who watch you, whether colleagues or children, are learning what love looks like by how you persist.

They're learning that commitment isn't emotion, but choice. That loyalty isn't loud, but enduring.

In that sense, endurance is the highest form of leadership, it teaches through time.

And grace is the melody that keeps the rhythm alive.

Self-Reflection

1. Where are you being invited to practice endurance instead of escape?

2. How can grace soften your discipline without weakening it?

3. Who around you might be learning faithfulness by watching how you persist?

Habits that Matter

- **The 90-Day Rhythm:** Choose one meaningful discipline, at work or home, and commit to it daily for 90 days. Keep a journal of the emotional journey, not just the outcomes.

- **Grace Reset:** When you fail a habit or miss a goal, respond with gentleness: reflect, reset, recommit, without self-condemnation.

- **Endurance Reflection:** Write a letter to your future self, describing the kind of steadiness you hope others remember.

- **Teach the Long View:** Share a story with your team or family about something that took you years to learn. Normalize slowness as wisdom.

Closing Thought

The long obedience is not glamorous. It rarely trends or shines. But it is where greatness quietly grows.

To endure is to love in time's direction, through fatigue, through change, through doubt. It's to hold a rhythm that others can rest upon.

Discipline may start with duty, but it ends in devotion. And grace, that quiet companion, ensures that even when you stumble, the rhythm continues.

Discipline is the steady rhythm of the FatherFrame™, the quiet consistency that makes leadership reliable, believable, and sustainable

So keep showing up. Keep staying true. Keep walking the long road with a steady step.

Because in the end, endurance isn't about outlasting others, it's about becoming more whole with every mile.

Consistency builds safety, but safety alone is not enough.

People need more than reliability; they need to feel understood. When discipline provides structure, compassion provides softness, the reminder that leadership is not only about guiding behaviors, but tending to hearts.

With your foundations steady, the next chapter invites you into the gentle power of empathy in action. This is where leadership shifts from managing outcomes to nurturing people.

Chapter Five – Compassion: The Power of Empathy in Action

"Compassion is not softness, it is the discipline of seeing people fully, responding with empathy, and leading in ways that restore dignity and unlock potential."

Compassion sits at the heart of human-centered leadership, transforming authority from something people fear into something they can rely on.

This chapter makes the case that empathy is not a soft extra, but a strategic advantage that fuels engagement, resilience, and loyalty. The way a parent comforts a child mirrors how a leader uplifts a struggling employee, by seeing beyond behavior to the unmet need beneath it. Compassion doesn't remove accountability; it makes accountability humane, and therefore sustainable. It is the force that keeps cultures healthy and relationships intact.

Compassion brings humanity into the FatherFrame™, reminding us that leadership is never simply about tasks, outcomes, or performance, it is always about people. When we learn to see beneath behavior, we shift from reacting to understanding. This chapter explores empathy as a strategic, relational, and restorative leadership force.

The Soft Strength

When I was younger, I believed leadership was about strength, visible, assertive, commanding.

I thought compassion was something optional, secondary, even indulgent, a trait for mentors and counsellors, not executives or decision-makers.

But years of leading people, raising children, and navigating failure taught me something profound: compassion *is* strength. Not the loud kind, not the kind that dominates a room, but the kind that keeps people from breaking when life gets heavy.

Compassion sits right at the heart of the FatherFramed™ Leadership Model, a reminder that effective leadership is always relational. When we understand the emotion beneath behavior, influence becomes human and lasting.

Compassion is strength under control, power restrained by love.

The Quiet Revolution of Kindness

There's a quiet revolution happening in leadership, a shift from dominance to empathy, from efficiency to humanity.

For decades, the corporate world equated toughness with effectiveness. But the research now confirms what the heart always knew: compassion drives performance far more sustainably than pressure ever could.

A 2022 Harvard Business Review study found that employees who described their managers as "compassionate" were 25% more engaged, 41% more loyal, and 31% more likely to report satisfaction in their roles.

The numbers tell the story: people don't leave jobs, they leave their manager, and often that means leaving the absence of empathy.

The same principle plays out in families. Children thrive not when they are controlled, but when they are understood. They mirror not the rules of their parents, but the tone of their compassion.

Kindness creates the safety from which courage grows.

The Strength to Stay Gentle
Gentleness is not weakness, it's wisdom matured.

It takes strength to stay calm when provoked, to listen when you'd rather instruct, to comfort when you're tired.

It takes strength to stay soft in a world that rewards sharp edges.

One of the most courageous things a leader can do is choose empathy when anger would be easier.

Years ago, I watched a senior leader respond to a costly mistake from one of his staff. It had financial repercussions, reputational risk, the kind of situation that usually triggers panic.

But instead of reacting, he said quietly, "Tell me what happened." His tone was calm, curious.

As the staff member explained, the tension dissolved. They found the root issue quickly, not incompetence, but miscommunication.

Afterward, I asked him how he stayed composed. He smiled and said, "People make fewer mistakes when they're not afraid to admit them."

That sentence became a cornerstone of my leadership, of my fathering.

Gentleness builds trust faster than authority ever could.

The Father's Heart
Fatherhood taught me this lesson in the most personal way.

When my son was ten, he was in tears after breaking our window with a soccer ball. His small shoulders trembled as he said, "I didn't mean to."

In that moment, I could have lectured him, about carelessness, consequences, responsibility. But something in his eyes, a mix of fear and shame, reminded me that compassion teaches better than correction.

So I knelt beside him, placed a hand on his shoulder, and said, "We'll fix it together."

The lesson stuck far deeper than a punishment ever would. Because compassion didn't erase accountability; it *accompanied* it.

The same principle holds in leadership. When a team member fails, the instinct to punish is natural, but the opportunity to teach is greater. The best leaders repair people, not just processes.

The Neuroscience of Compassion
Modern neuroscience reveals that compassion is hardwired into us.

When we witness someone suffering, the brain's mirror neurons activate, we feel what they feel. That's why empathy can be exhausting; our bodies experience a shadow of another's pain.

But compassion goes beyond empathy. Empathy *feels* with others; compassion *acts* for them.

Research from Stanford University shows that compassion training not only increases emotional resilience but also improves decision-making under stress.
Compassion calms the amygdala (the brain's threat center) and activates the prefrontal cortex, the part responsible for rational thinking and ethical judgment.

In other words, compassion literally makes us wiser.

This science confirms what every parent already knows, love steadies the nervous system. A calm voice, a gentle presence, a reassuring touch: these simple gestures regulate chaos into clarity.

When leaders act with compassion, they do more than soothe emotion; they unlock cognition. Teams think better when they feel safe.

Courage in Compassion

To truly lead with compassion, you have to let the walls down. You have to feel others' pain, their fear, their doubt. You have to risk being affected.That's what makes compassion hard: it's costly. It asks for your emotional availability when you'd rather protect yourself.

But here's the paradox, the leaders who dare to care end up the strongest. They build cultures that can withstand crisis because trust becomes their infrastructure.

In family life, compassion builds the same resilience. Children who are shown consistent empathy grow into adults who can handle hardship without cynicism. They learn that mistakes don't end love, they invite growth.

The same holds for teams. Compassion doesn't make people soft; it makes them secure. And secure people perform with creativity and courage.

Compassion as Leadership's Greatest Discipline

We often think of compassion as spontaneous, an emotional response. But in reality, compassion is a discipline.

It means choosing understanding over judgment.
It means holding space when your instinct is to fix.
It means staying kind when stress makes you sharp.

The strongest leaders and fathers I know practice compassion *deliberately*. They make it part of their daily rhythm, to pause before responding, to seek context before conclusion.

Compassion isn't natural; it's nurtured. It grows through self-awareness, humility, and practice.

And the result is transformative: teams trust you, children confide in you, and your influence extends far beyond your authority.

As Maya Angelou stated so beautifully "I've learned that people will forget what you said, people will forget what you did, but people will never forget how you made them feel", and compassion is the feeling that lasts.

Self-Reflection

1. When was the last time you chose compassion over correction? What changed because of it?

2. How does your leadership culture, or your family's tone, reflect your capacity for gentleness under pressure?

3. What boundaries do you need to set to ensure compassion doesn't turn into exhaustion?

Habits that Matter

- **Pause Before Power:** When tempted to assert authority, pause and ask, "What does this person need right now, fear or understanding?"

- **Compassion Audit:** Reflect on three recent interactions. Did your tone create safety or stress?

- **Reframe Mistakes:** Replace "What's wrong with you?" with "What happened to you?" or "What support do you need?"

- **Daily Kindness:** Practice one intentional act of kindness at work or home, small, specific, and unseen.

Seeing with the Heart

There's a difference between *looking* and *seeing*.

Looking is mechanical, a transaction between the eyes and the brain.

Seeing is moral, a meeting between souls.

To see with the heart is to look past the surface and witness the truth beneath: the tiredness behind the smile, the courage beneath the failure, the story that explains the behavior. It's to see others not as objects in your orbit, but as sacred beings carrying their own unseen battles.

Leadership and fatherhood both demand this kind of sight, not the sight that judges, but the sight that understands.

Because people blossom when they are seen, and they wither when they are invisible.

The Gift of Being Seen

I remember once walking into a meeting where a junior staff member was presenting for the first time. She'd prepared meticulously, but you could see the nerves in her hands. As she spoke, the room buzzed with side conversations, phones, laptops, distraction.

Halfway through, I stopped the meeting. "Let's give her our full attention," I said gently. "She's earned it."

The room went silent. She continued, steadier this time. When she finished, the applause was genuine.

Later, she told me, "That moment changed how I see myself."

All I did was *see her*. But for her, that sight became validation, the permission to take up space.

That's the power of being seen. It doesn't inflate ego; it restores worth.

And the reverse is just as true: invisibility erodes identity. When people feel unseen, they begin to shrink, to disengage, to doubt their value.

The best leaders and parents understand that their first duty is not to manage or to teach, it's to notice.

The Eyes of Compassion
To see with the heart requires slowing down, because speed is the enemy of empathy.

When we rush, we reduce people to roles: the colleague, the client, the child, the spouse. But when we pause long enough to *notice,* the human behind the role reappears.

There's a reason why the ancient word for compassion, *splagchnizomai* in Greek, literally means "to be moved by deep, visceral compassion for another's suffering, as if feeling it in one's gut or bowels." It describes a visceral response, not an intellectual one. True compassion doesn't happen from a distance; it moves you inside.

I once met an Aged Care Nurse who told me, "My job isn't to heal the dying; it's to make sure they're not invisible."
That sentence has haunted me ever since, and reshaped how I led in that industry.

In business, we often forget that beneath every title is a human being craving acknowledgment. We measure performance but overlook presence. We praise outcomes but forget the effort.

To see with the heart is to reverse that order.

It's to notice the humanity before the hierarchy.

The Father's Gaze

Children read their parents' faces long before they understand their words.

When a child enters the room, they search instinctively for cues, *Am I welcome here? Am I seen?*

I once came home from work frustrated and distracted. My son ran to show me something he'd built with Lego. Without looking up from my phone, I murmured, "That's great, buddy."

He paused, then quietly walked away.

That night, guilt sank deep. I'd been present in body but absent in spirit. He hadn't needed my words, he'd needed my *eyes*.

The next day, I tried again. I put the phone down, crouched to his level, and said, "Show me." He beamed.

It lasted two minutes, but those two minutes repaired something.

Fatherhood, I've learned, is the daily art of seeing your children as if for the first time.

Leadership is no different. When you look at your team with that same attentive gaze, when you notice their effort, their fatigue, their humanity, you communicate dignity without saying a word.

People become their best selves under the warmth of recognition.

Seeing Beyond Behavior

To see with the heart also means seeing beyond behavior, to the story that shaped it.

When someone lashes out, withdraws, or underperforms, it's easy to label them: "difficult," "lazy," "unmotivated." But those are surface words for deeper realities.

In my years managing teams, I've learned that nearly every performance issue is, at its core, a *pain issue*.
A personal struggle, a hidden grief, a fear of failure.

One man on my team once missed multiple deadlines. I was ready to address it directly, until I asked how he was doing. Tears came instantly. He was separating from his wife.

That conversation changed everything. I didn't lower expectations, but I adjusted compassion.

Seeing with the heart doesn't excuse poor behavior, but it contextualizes it. It lets you lead from understanding rather than assumption.

And it's not limited to the workplace. Families thrive when we learn to look past the immediate and ask, *What's this behavior protecting? What pain is it trying to express?*

Children act out not because they're defiant, but because they're overwhelmed. Employees disengage not because they're lazy, but because they feel unseen.

Compassion doesn't lower standards, it raises connection.

The Practice of Attentive Presence
To see with the heart is an act of attention, and attention is love made visible.

When you truly listen, your attention becomes healing. You don't even have to fix anything; your presence itself becomes a mirror in which others rediscover their worth.

There's a sacred stillness that descends when someone feels fully seen. It's as if time slows, defenses drop, and the truth of who they are rises to the surface.

I've had conversations where words barely mattered, where a long pause, an empathetic nod, or a shared silence did more than any advice could.

In that moment, the person feels something primal and holy: *I exist. I matter. I am not alone.*

In a distracted age, attention is the rarest form of generosity.

That's why I often tell leaders and parents alike: your greatest gift is not your guidance; it's your gaze.

The Vision That Transforms
Seeing with the heart transforms not just how you treat others, but how you perceive the world itself.

You begin to notice beauty in the ordinary, the colleague who always stays late without complaint, the child humming to themselves, the stranger offering a quiet kindness.

You start to live awake, aware that everyone is carrying something you can't see, and that small gestures of empathy might be the only light they receive today.

This vision changes culture. Teams become kinder. Homes become softer. The world becomes, in small but measurable ways, more human.

And it all begins with eyes that choose to see differently.

Self-Reflection

1. Who in your life might be feeling unseen, and how could you change that this week?

2. What behaviors or attitudes in others could you reinterpret through the lens of compassion rather than judgment?

3. When was the last time someone truly *saw* you, and how did it change you?

Habits that Matter

- **The Two-Minute Rule:** Each day, give someone your full, undistracted attention for two minutes. No phone, no multitasking. Just presence.

- **Notice the Invisible:** Make a point to acknowledge someone who often goes unnoticed, a cleaner, receptionist, or quiet team member.

- **Reframe Reaction:** Before reacting to a mistake or conflict, ask, "What story might I be missing here?"

- **Family Eye Contact:** When you greet your loved ones, look them in the eyes for a moment longer than usual. Let your gaze say what words can't.

Leading with Empathy

Empathy is often spoken about as though it's a feeling, something soft and sentimental, like sympathy dressed in leadership language.

But real empathy is not fragile; it's fierce.
It's the ability to enter another person's world without losing your footing in your own. It's emotional intelligence translated into practical, relational courage.

In both leadership and fatherhood, empathy is not an accessory, it's the architecture. It builds trust, dissolves fear, and transforms compliance into commitment.

To lead with empathy is to lead with the whole heart, perceptive, responsive, and strong enough to hold another's perspective without collapsing your own.

The Anatomy of Empathy
At its core, empathy has three dimensions:

1. **Cognitive empathy**, understanding what someone feels and why.

2. **Emotional empathy**, sharing their feeling, resonating with their experience.

3. **Compassionate empathy**, acting on that understanding to alleviate suffering or support growth.

Leaders often stop at the first. They understand *intellectually* what someone feels but rarely act upon it. But true empathy is not complete until it moves, until it changes something in the way we lead, decide, or respond.

In my early years of management, I mistook awareness for empathy. I noticed when people were struggling, but I didn't adjust. I assumed insight alone was enough.

Then one day, a team member came to me after a long meeting and said, "You listen really well, but nothing ever changes."

That comment humbled me. I realized that empathy without action is observation; empathy with action is leadership.

The Leadership Power of Emotional Attunement

People don't expect their leaders to be therapists. They don't need you to solve every problem. They need to know that their inner world matters to you, that their humanity is not a liability to the organization's goals.

When a leader can name what others feel, "I can see that this decision frustrates you," or "It sounds like you're feeling undervalued", tension defuses instantly. Naming emotion is one of the most powerful acts of validation. It tells people: *I see you, and your feelings are legitimate.*

The psychologist Daniel Goleman, who popularized the concept of *emotional intelligence*, found that the best-performing leaders consistently score high in empathy. But not because they're "nice", because they understand that emotion is data.

Emotion tells you what's really happening beneath the metrics.

In family life, this same skill is transformational. When your child storms out or withdraws, empathy says, "Something's hurting," not "You're being disrespectful." When you meet emotion with understanding, the battle ends before it begins.

Accountability Through Understanding

There's a misconception that empathy weakens accountability. That if we "understand too much," we'll let standards slide. But in reality, empathy strengthens accountability because it roots it in respect.

A leader who leads with empathy doesn't avoid truth, they deliver it in a way that can be heard.

I once had to address consistent underperformance in a team member. Before diving into targets and metrics, I asked, "How are you, really?" The conversation revealed not truly understanding their role, how they add value and fear of letting others down. We adjusted workload temporarily, clarified expectations, and created small wins to rebuild confidence.

Performance improved dramatically, not because I lowered the bar, but because empathy built trust strong enough to support honesty.

Empathy doesn't mean excusing behavior. It means addressing it humanely. It allows for feedback that uplifts rather than humiliates.

Accountability delivered through empathy sounds like:

- "I value you too much not to tell you this."

- "You're capable of more, and I'm here to help you get there."

This combination of compassion and candor is what separates leaders people follow from leaders people fear.

The Father's Parallel
Parenting offers the purest laboratory for empathy in action.

When my daughter was a teenager, she went through a season of defiance, nothing dramatic, but full of small resistances: late homework, eye rolls, closed doors. My instinct was to correct. To tighten rules.

But correction without connection only widens the gap.

One night, instead of lecturing, I sat outside her door and said softly, "I know life feels heavy right now. I just want you to know I'm here."

Silence at first. Then, after a few minutes, she opened the door and whispered, "I know."

That tiny moment shifted everything. The rules stayed, but the relationship healed.

The same principle applies to teams. Empathy doesn't mean lowering standards, it means raising your relational investment.

When people feel seen and respected, they often hold themselves to higher standards than you ever could impose.

Empathy builds self-accountability through dignity.

Empathy as Strategic Advantage
Empathy is often categorized as a "soft skill," but it produces hard results.

Empathetic leaders read the emotional landscape accurately, they can sense morale dips before they show up in metrics. They spot burnout early. They anticipate conflict.

Companies led by empathetic executives consistently outperform competitors in engagement, innovation, and retention. It's not magic; it's neurobiology. Safety unleashes creativity. When people feel understood, their prefrontal cortex, the brain's decision-making center, stays active. When they feel threatened, it shuts down.

That's why fear-based cultures may get short-term compliance, but never long-term brilliance.

Empathy, strategically applied, is the difference between employees working *for* you and working *with* you.

And it's not just corporate. Families, too, thrive on emotional safety. Children raised in empathetic environments grow into adults capable of collaboration and courage, because they learned early that vulnerability isn't danger, it's connection.

Empathy with Boundaries

To lead with empathy does not mean absorbing everyone's pain. That's compassion fatigue, the burnout that comes from carrying what isn't yours to carry.

Empathy requires boundaries. You can be fully present without being consumed. You can understand without rescuing.

One executive I coached as a Emotional Intelligence Coach had developed severe burnout from her "open-door policy." She listened to everyone's problems, late nights, weekends, constant emotional triage. She was loved but depleted.

We worked on boundaries: setting specific hours for check-ins, delegating mentoring, and separating care from control. Within months, her energy returned, and her team's autonomy grew.

Boundaries don't limit empathy; they protect it.

Think of empathy like a lantern, it shines brighter when protected by glass. Without boundaries, the flame burns out.

The Courage to Lead People, Not Performance

At its core, empathy requires courage, because it demands you slow down enough to feel. It's easier to measure output than to understand emotion. Easier to chase numbers than to nurture souls.

But leading people, not performance, means recognizing that productivity is the fruit, not the root. The root is relationship.

When people trust you, they bring you their best ideas, their creativity, their truth. Without empathy, they give you only compliance, the minimal exchange of energy for money.

Leadership without empathy is management. Leadership with empathy is ministry, the stewardship of human potential.

And that's what the world, and our children, need most right now: not more control, but more care.

Self-Reflection

1. When was the last time you led with empathy instead of authority? What changed in the outcome?

2. How might empathy transform your approach to accountability and feedback?

3. What boundaries could you set to sustain empathy without exhaustion?

Habits that Matter

- **Empathy Mapping:** Before your next one-on-one, ask: What might this person be feeling, fearing, and hoping for? Prepare your tone accordingly.

- **Emotion Naming:** Practice naming emotions aloud in meetings: "I sense some tension, let's talk about it." This normalizes honesty.

- **Boundary Setting:** Define when and how you'll be emotionally available, and communicate that clearly.

- **Empathy Pause:** Before reacting, take a single breath and ask, "What else might be true here?"

The Cost of Caring

Compassion has a shadow. It is luminous and life-giving, but it can also quietly exhaust the very heart that offers it. To care deeply, truly, fully, is to open yourself to a kind of exposure most people avoid. Every act of empathy, every shared sorrow, every emotional burden taken on comes at a price.

And yet, we rarely talk about the toll. We celebrate kindness, but not the fatigue it breeds. We applaud servant leadership, but not the silent depletion that can follow.

To sustain compassion in the long run, both as leaders and as parents, we must confront this truth: you cannot pour from an empty cup.

The Hidden Weight of Empathy

Empathy asks us to enter another person's emotional landscape, to feel what they feel, to see the world through their eyes. Done too often, or without boundaries, that landscape can begin to eclipse our own.

I've met countless leaders who burn out not from overwork, but from *over-caring*. They internalize every staff member's anxiety, every family conflict, every organizational struggle. They become emotional reservoirs, absorbing everyone else's pain until there's no room left for joy.

Neuroscience explains why. Empathetic resonance triggers the same neural networks that fire when we personally experience pain. The brain doesn't fully distinguish between witnessing suffering and enduring it.

That's why compassion fatigue is so real. It's not moral weakness; it's biology.

And yet, the solution isn't to harden the heart. It's to *strengthen the vessel*.

Empathy must be managed like any other finite resource, replenished, renewed, respected.

When Caring Becomes Compulsion

There's a subtle point where empathy stops being service and starts being compulsion, where caring for others becomes a way to avoid caring for ourselves.

I remember a time early in my leadership career when I prided myself on being available 24/7. Every text answered. Every crisis absorbed. I thought that was integrity, proof of dedication.

But it wasn't. It was fear. Fear of being seen as detached. Fear of letting people down.

One night, after yet another late call, my daughter said, "Dad, you always sound kinder to work people than to us."

That cut deeper than any board critique could.

In that moment, I realized something crucial: my compassion was no longer balanced. I was giving generously outward, but offering nothing inward.

Unbalanced compassion eventually mutates into resentment. You start to feel drained, then bitter, then numb. And when numbness arrives, you've crossed from empathy to exhaustion.

Real compassion cannot thrive where self-respect has been abandoned.

The Myth of Selfless Service

The phrase "selfless service" sounds noble, but it's dangerously incomplete.

True service is not selfless; it's *self-aware*.

To serve sustainably, you must protect the instrument of your service, your body, your mind, your emotional energy.

There's a story of a humanitarian doctor who worked in war zones for decades. When asked how he avoided burnout, he said, "I learned to see suffering as sacred, but not mine to own. My job is to stand near it, not inside it."

That's the essence of healthy empathy: *proximity without absorption.*

It's the same wisdom every seasoned parent eventually learns. You can walk beside your child through pain, but you cannot carry their entire world. To try is to break under love's own weight.

Caring doesn't mean collapsing.

The Discipline of Renewal
Leaders, like nurses often forget that rest is not optional, it's obedience to a deeper rhythm. Even the most compassionate heart has limits, and respecting those limits is not selfishness; it's stewardship.

One executive I coached used to end every day with a "compassion debrief." She'd mentally release the stories and emotions she'd absorbed, sometimes journaling or walking in silence. "If I don't put them down," she said, "they follow me into sleep."

This practice saved her from burnout. It allowed her to continue leading with empathy without being consumed by it.

For me, renewal often comes through stillness, walking with my chickens, cooking, or simply waking up without an agenda. These quiet rituals wash the residue of other people's pain from my spirit.

Leaders who never pause become brittle. Parents who never rest become reactive. Renewal is the soil where compassion regrows.

As a new parent, I always said that I could deal with anything, as long as the baby sleeps and I get a good nights sleep.

And yet, renewal requires humility, the courage to admit that you are not infinite.

Grace for the Giver
Those who care the most are often the hardest on themselves. They forgive others easily but offer themselves no mercy.

But compassion, if it is to endure, must include self-compassion.

Self-compassion doesn't mean indulgence. It means acknowledging your humanity with the same tenderness you offer others. It's speaking to yourself like someone you love.

When I catch myself spiraling into guilt for what I *should* have done, for the meeting I cut short, the phone call I missed, the moment I snapped, I try to hear the voice I would use for a friend in the same position.

It always sounds gentler.

That's grace: the reminder that you are not the savior, only the servant. The work is never entirely yours to finish, but you are called to give your portion faithfully, then rest.

Grace doesn't erase responsibility; it replenishes capacity.

Learning to Let Go
Perhaps the hardest lesson for those who lead with empathy is learning when to release.

There comes a point when holding someone's pain becomes unhelpful, when continuing to carry it deprives them of their own growth.

A wise leader or parent knows when to step back and let life itself take over as teacher. That restraint is not detachment; it's respect.

I once had a brilliant young manager in my team, who faced repeated setbacks. I spent hours coaching, encouraging, troubleshooting. But at some point, I realized my help had become dependency. He wasn't growing; he was leaning.

So I stepped back, gently but firmly. "You've got this," I said. "You know what to do."

He did. He stumbled, recovered, and found his confidence.

That's when I learned that real compassion doesn't just rescue, it *releases*.

Love strong enough to let go is the most mature form of empathy.

The Sacred Balance
Compassion lives in tension, between care and containment, empathy and endurance.
You cannot sustain one without the other.

It's like breathing: inhale others' stories, exhale your own peace. Receive, respond, release.

The rhythm of sustainable compassion is not a straight line of giving; it's a circle of exchange.

When you care for others, let others care for you. When you listen deeply, take time to be silent for yourself. When you lead with empathy, lead yourself with equal gentleness.

That's how compassion remains power instead of burden.

Because in the end, the world doesn't need martyrs of empathy; it needs *models of wholeness.*

People who prove that you can care deeply without collapsing, give generously without losing, love fully without forgetting yourself.

Self-Reflection

1. In what ways has your empathy turned into emotional overextension?

2. What practices could you build to renew yourself after heavy days of caring?

3. Are you carrying pain that isn't yours to carry anymore?

Habits that Matter

- **Emotional Debrief:** At the end of each day, name what isn't yours to carry and consciously let it go.

- **Compassion Boundary:** Write a short mantra, "I can care deeply and still rest." Repeat it when you feel overextended.

- **Scheduled Silence:** Block 15 minutes each day with no phone, no task, no input, only stillness.

- **Circle of Care:** Identify two people who pour into you. Schedule time with them this week, not as duty, but as replenishment.

Compassion as Culture

Every leader eventually realizes that compassion cannot remain personal.

It must travel, from the individual to the collective, from the heart of one to the heartbeat of many.

A compassionate organization, a compassionate family, a compassionate community, these are not accidents of personality. They are cultures built by intention.

And while empathy begins in the private realm of emotion, compassion, empathy in motion, becomes transformative only when it shapes systems, not just sentiments.

Kindness, when structured, becomes strategy.

From Individual Virtue to Collective Strength

Most leaders underestimate how profoundly their personal tone echoes through a culture.

The way you greet your team in the morning becomes how they greet each other.

The patience you show in conflict becomes the emotional standard for disagreement.

The generosity you model in private becomes the currency of public trust.

Culture is not written in values statements or policy manuals, it's composed in the thousand small moments that people witness daily.

I once visited a nonprofit with an extraordinary reputation for morale. The secret wasn't perks or pay, it was tone. Every meeting began with gratitude. Every mistake was treated as a lesson, not a liability.

When I asked the CEO how they sustained it, she said, "We don't teach compassion; we imitate it."

That's culture: when the leader's heart becomes the organization's default setting.

The Architecture of a Compassionate Workplace

Building compassion into organizational DNA requires more than emotional intelligence; it takes design.

Compassion needs structure, policies, rhythms, rituals, to ensure it endures beyond personalities.

Some of the most effective practices I've seen include:

- **Transparent Communication:** Openly discussing challenges and emotions normalizes vulnerability and dismantles shame.

- **Listening Systems:** Anonymous feedback loops or listening sessions where employees feel heard without fear of reprisal.

- **Kind Accountability:** Performance reviews that include not only outcomes, but also how people treated each other in achieving them.

- **Restorative Practices:** After conflict or failure, focusing on repair rather than blame.

- **Wellbeing Embedded, Not Added:** Compassionate cultures don't bolt on "wellness" programs, they embed rest, flexibility, and mental health into how work happens.

These aren't soft luxuries; they are hard infrastructure for sustainable excellence.

Because compassion and performance are not opposites, they are partners. One fuels the other.

The Business Case for Humanity

There was a time when talking about compassion in corporate boardrooms drew polite smiles and quiet skepticism. Those days are fading.

Empirical evidence now supports what ancient wisdom has always known: kindness is not only moral, it's profitable.

Studies from Deloitte, Gallup, and Oxford University show that companies with compassionate cultures outperform competitors in retention, innovation, and resilience. Teams with empathetic leaders report higher trust, lower turnover, and stronger creativity under pressure.

This isn't sentimental theory, it's strategy.

Because in an era of automation and artificial intelligence, the human differentiator is emotional intelligence. Machines can calculate; only humans can care.

When people feel psychologically safe, they take risks, share ideas, and admit mistakes early, all vital to innovation. When fear dominates, creativity dies.

That's why the most forward-thinking CEOs are becoming chief empathy officers, not out of altruism, but survival. In a volatile, uncertain world, compassion is the ultimate stabilizer.

Kindness as Operational Excellence

I once worked at an organization that reduced staff turnover by 40% in a single year, not through pay rises, but through culture reform.

The new director introduced one simple rule: *"We treat everyone as though they're doing their best."*

That statement transformed everything. Conversations became gentler, assumptions kinder, mistakes more openly addressed. Productivity rose not because expectations lowered, but because trust replaced fear.

When compassion becomes policy, efficiency follows. People no longer waste energy defending themselves or hiding flaws. The organization's emotional friction drops, freeing capacity for creativity and service.

In a family, the same principle applies.
A household ruled by constant criticism may function, but it never flourishes. A home grounded in compassion operates with quiet ease, conflicts resolve faster, communication deepens, affection flows naturally.

Kindness is not the opposite of structure; it is the oil that keeps structure from grinding.

Scaling Humanity Without Losing Soul

As organizations grow, compassion often dilutes. What began as relational can become transactional.

To prevent this, leaders must design empathy into scale.
That means creating systems that *remember people*.

I've seen large companies use "Human Moments", brief check-ins at the start of meetings to ask how people are *really* doing.

Others schedule "empathy weeks," where executives spend time shadowing frontline staff, listening rather than speaking.

In families, it looks like setting intentional rituals of connection, dinner without devices, walks that invite conversation, a bedtime question like, "What was good today?"

These small, structured moments keep humanity visible amid complexity.

Scaling compassion isn't about sentimentality; it's about design fidelity, ensuring the culture's emotional DNA stays intact as it multiplies.

The Leader as Cultural Mirror

Leaders are mirrors. They don't create culture; they reveal it.

When you walk through an office or home, you can sense immediately what kind of compassion lives there, whether it's genuine or performative, whether kindness flows freely or is rationed.

That atmosphere is not accidental; it's a reflection of leadership tone.

A leader who responds with empathy during crisis teaches an entire organization how to stay humane under stress. A father who apologizes when he's wrong teaches his children that humility and authority can coexist.

Every time you choose compassion over control, you rewire the culture's emotional memory.

Over time, those choices accumulate into a legacy.

The Moral Horizon of Compassion

At its highest level, compassion becomes not just practice, but principle, a moral horizon that shapes every decision.

It asks hard questions:

- How does this policy affect the most vulnerable?

- Does this decision preserve dignity as well as profit?

- Are we growing at the expense of humanity, or because of it?

When compassion informs governance, organizations transcend efficiency and enter integrity. They stop asking, "What can we get away with?" and start asking, "What would love require here?"

That single shift, from advantage to stewardship, marks the difference between success and significance.

Compassion, scaled wisely, becomes not a tactic, but a testimony.

The Legacy of Kindness

In time, all structures decay, all metrics fade. What endures is how people felt under your leadership.

They will forget the quarterly results, but they will remember the tone of your voice.

They will forget the projects, but not the way you made them feel safe to fail, free to speak, proud to belong.

That memory becomes the emotional architecture of the next generation.

Your compassion becomes their culture.

That's how love scales, not through slogans or strategies, but through consistency. One person at a time, one act at a time, until care itself becomes contagious.

And when compassion becomes reflex, not reaction, that's when culture has fully transformed.

Self-Reflection

1. How does compassion currently show up, or fail to show up, in your workplace or home culture?

2. What small rituals could you introduce to make empathy habitual, not exceptional?

3. How might your leadership mirror the kind of humanity you want others to emulate?

Habits that Matter

- **Culture Audit:** Review your team or household routines. Identify where fear or criticism replaces kindness. Redesign one practice through compassion.

- **Ritualize Empathy:** Begin each meeting or meal with a gratitude or check-in moment.

- **Feedback Through Care:** Before giving feedback, ask, "What tone will build this person's dignity as well as their skill?"

- **Kindness Cascade:** Each week, name one act of compassion you observed. Share it publicly. Make kindness visible.

Closing Thought

Compassion begins as an act. It becomes a habit. Eventually, it matures into atmosphere.

When kindness permeates systems, trust becomes default, creativity flourishes, and the organization, or family, begins to hum with quiet strength.

Compassion deepens the FatherFrame™ by grounding leadership in empathy, humanity, and the courage to see beneath the surface. That is the true power of empathy in action: not just to heal individuals, but to humanize the whole.

Caring for people requires courage: the courage to be whole, to live aligned, to close the gap between what you say and what you do. When empathy softens the ground, integrity strengthens the roots.

The next chapter explores how being the same person everywhere, at work, at home, under pressure, and in private, shapes a form of leadership that people can trust not just in good seasons, but in the hardest ones.

Chapter Six — Integrity: The Courage to Stay Whole

"Integrity is the alignment of character and behavior, when who you are matches how you lead, trust becomes inevitable."

Integrity is what allows people to trust your leadership even when the pressure rises. In this chapter, integrity is defined not as perfection, but as wholeness, the alignment between your values, decisions, and behavior. Whether at home or in the boardroom, people instinctively follow leaders who are the same person everywhere.

This chapter explores how integrity builds psychological safety, strengthens culture, and creates the kind of leader whose presence brings clarity rather than confusion. Without integrity, nothing in leadership is sustainable; with it, almost anything is possible.

Integrity is the aligning pillar of the FatherFrame™, the bond between character and conduct that makes leadership believable. More than honesty, it is wholeness: being the same person in every room. This chapter examines how integrity builds trust that lasts beyond moments, decisions, or circumstances.

The Seam Between Words and Actions

Integrity begins at the seam, the place where words and actions meet.

It's not measured by what we say when people are watching, but by what we choose when no one is.

In both leadership and family life, integrity is the unseen architecture holding everything together. It's what makes promises trustworthy, relationships safe, and cultures stable.

And yet, integrity is often misunderstood. We think of it as moral rigidity, a refusal to bend. But real integrity isn't hardness; it's coherence. It's the internal harmony that allows a person to remain consistent even in contradiction.

Integrity means being the same person through every season, consistent in values, adaptable in method, truthful in both victory and failure.

It's not about never falling short. It's about refusing to pretend when you do.

The Foundation of Wholeness

The word *integrity* comes from the Latin *integer*, meaning "whole," "complete," or "undivided."

It suggests that to live with integrity is to live without fragmentation, without the exhausting divide between who we are privately and what we present publicly.

That's why dishonesty feels so heavy; it splits us. When our words and actions diverge, the soul experiences a kind of moral vertigo, we lose our balance.

I learned this lesson not from a mentor or a manager, but from my daughter. She was eight, and I had promised to attend her school concert. A last-minute meeting ran over, and I arrived just as the lights dimmed, too late.

She didn't say anything, but her small silence carried a verdict. I had meant well, but I hadn't kept my word.

That night, as I tucked her in, I said, "I'm sorry." She smiled faintly and said, "It's okay, Dad. You're busy."

But it wasn't okay. Integrity had cost me something that day, not my reputation, but her quiet confidence in my reliability.

I've never forgotten that feeling. Because integrity isn't a public performance; it's a private covenant.

Leadership's Double Exposure

Every leader lives in a kind of double exposure: the visible and the invisible.

There's the version that people see, confident, decisive, articulate, and the private version that wrestles with doubt, ego, fatigue, and fear.

Integrity doesn't erase that tension; it reconciles it. It refuses to let the external outrun the internal.

The corporate world often rewards results, not character. But every sustainable success is built on moral infrastructure. When leaders compromise small truths for quick wins, they start eroding that foundation grain by grain, until the structure looks fine from the outside but is hollow within.

The irony is that people can sense it. They may not articulate it, but they *feel* when a leader's words lack congruence with reality. Culture picks up hypocrisy like radar.

A leader's integrity is the organization's emotional thermostat. When you're honest about your limits, others learn to trust their own. When you own mistakes publicly, you create safety for transparency.

Integrity doesn't demand perfection from others, it models honesty about imperfection.

The Father's Example
In the home, integrity takes on its most intimate form.

Children are master observers. They may not yet have the language for hypocrisy, but they can smell it. They notice when tone contradicts teaching, when a parent preaches patience but practices irritation, or promises time but gives leftovers.

But they also notice when humility shows up, when an adult apologizes, admits wrong, or stays gentle under pressure. Those moments become moral anchors.

I once apologized to my son after losing my temper over something trivial. He looked surprised, as though adults weren't supposed to admit failure. Later that week, I overheard him telling his sister, "It's okay to say sorry."

That's how integrity multiplies, through small acts of honesty that echo beyond their moment.

The best lesson you can give your children, or your team, is the example of congruence: the assurance that what you say and who you are belong to the same story.

Integrity in the Mundane
Integrity doesn't only live in the big ethical crossroads, the public scandals or moral dilemmas. It lives in the mundane decisions no one sees.

Returning the extra change.

Telling the full truth when a partial one would suffice.
Keeping a small promise even when no one would notice if you didn't.

It's in those quiet moments that character calibrates itself.

The daily practice of integrity is like tuning an instrument. Each honest act keeps you in harmony; each compromise creates dissonance.

Integrity, like fitness, is built through repetition. It's not a singular virtue; it's a sustained rhythm, the habit of truth, practiced until it becomes muscle memory.

The Moral Simplicity of Truth
The beautiful thing about integrity is its simplicity. Once you decide to be whole, decisions become clearer.

Truth may not always be easy, but it is uncomplicated.

Dishonesty, by contrast, multiplies complexity, every lie demands another to sustain it. Leaders who compromise truth spend more time managing perceptions than solving problems.

Integrity frees energy. When your words match your heart, you stop performing and start leading.

Self-Reflection
1. Where do your words and actions feel out of alignment, even subtly?

2. What's one small promise you could keep this week to rebuild trust in that area?

3. Who in your life has modelled integrity not through perfection, but through honesty?

Habits that Matter

- **The Alignment Audit:** Write down your top five values. For each, note one way your daily actions reflect or contradict it.

- **Micro-Honesty:** Practise telling the full truth in a small, low-stakes moment. Feel how much lighter it is.

- **Public Apology:** Choose one area, at home or work, where you fell short. Name it aloud, without excuses.

- **Integrity Anchor:** End your day by asking, "Did my actions today match my intentions?"

The Pressure Test

Integrity is easy when the sun is shining. It's in the storm that its true shape appears.

Every leader, every parent, every human being eventually faces what I call *the pressure test*, that moment when doing what's right will cost you something tangible: time, money, approval, comfort, or reputation.

And it's in that crucible that the inner scaffolding of your life is revealed.

Integrity isn't forged in quiet reflection alone. It's proved in the moment when the easier path whispers your name, and you choose the harder truth instead.

The Moment of Decision

I remember once leading a team under severe financial strain. We were closing the quarter short, and one executive suggested a "creative" reclassification of revenue, technically legal, morally grey. It would have smoothed the report, bought breathing space, even earned applause.

I felt the pull of rationalization: *It's harmless... it's temporary... it's for the greater good.*

But something inside me resisted, not out of fear of getting caught, but from a quieter conviction: if I bend the truth here, I'll spend years trying to stand upright again.

We reported honestly. The results looked ugly, the conversation with the board was uncomfortable, but the relief was immense. The team knew, without a word, that we had chosen integrity over image.

That moment redefined trust across the organization. It became a reference point, the story people told newcomers when describing our culture.

Integrity costs in the short term. But dishonesty costs forever.

The Anatomy of Temptation
Temptation doesn't usually announce itself as evil. It arrives disguised as practicality.

You'll hear it in sentences like:

- "It's just this once."

- "Everyone does it."

- "No one will notice."

- "I don't have a choice."

Every compromise begins with a justification.

But integrity, at its simplest, is refusing to let circumstance dictate conscience. It's remembering that every small choice tilts the arc of your character, toward wholeness or fracture.

The psychologist Albert Bandura described this as *moral disengagement*, the process by which we convince ourselves that wrong is right through clever language.

We rename deceit as *strategy*, pride as *confidence*, greed as *ambition*.

And each linguistic sleight of hand pulls us further from truth.

The antidote? Conscious awareness. Naming temptation for what it is before it shapes us unseen.

Stress and the Split Self

Pressure doesn't just tempt us to lie outwardly, it divides us inwardly.

Under stress, the mind seeks shortcuts. We begin compartmentalizing: professional self, personal self, moral self.

We tell ourselves that compromise at work doesn't affect our integrity at home, that a white lie in the office won't echo in the family.

But character doesn't operate in silos. The fracture of integrity in one arena eventually seeps into all others.

I once worked for a CEO who confided, "I feel like two people, the one my family loves and the one my board expects."

He was exhausted, not from workload, but from duality.

We talked together about aligning his values and behavior until he could lead from a single self again.

Within months, his energy returned. Integrity had healed the internal split.

Because that's what it does, it integrates. It gathers all the fragmented versions of you and says, *Be one.*

The Leadership Paradox: Pressure and Perception

In leadership, integrity is often tested not just by private temptation but by public perception.

There's a cruel irony in success, the higher you rise, the more others project onto you, and the harder it becomes to admit weakness. You start managing the myth of yourself rather than the truth.

I once caught myself editing my words in an executive meeting to sound more confident than I felt. It was harmless enough, until it became habit.

Gradually, I noticed a disconnect between what I felt and what I presented.

That's how integrity erodes, not in a single betrayal, but through incremental pretense.

It takes humility, and courage, to break that cycle. To say, "I don't know," "I was wrong," or "I need help."

Those words cost ego, but they buy trust.

Authenticity, not invincibility, is what makes a leader credible under pressure.

The Family Mirror
Home has a way of reflecting who we really are under stress.

It's easy to preach patience, empathy, or calm when the world is orderly. But when fatigue, deadlines, or frustration spill into the evening, the cracks appear.

I've lost count of how many times I've snapped at loved ones over something trivial, only to feel shame creep in moments later.

Integrity in the home is not about being perfect; it's about being transparent. It's about owning those failures before they calcify into patterns.

One evening, after a particularly hard day, I apologised to my family for my tone at dinner. I expected dismissal or discomfort, but instead, my daughter said, "That must have been a hard day, Dad."

In that instant, the pressure dissolved. Integrity had transformed tension into connection.

Our children learn far more from how we handle pressure than how we handle success.

The Pressure of Approval
Perhaps the subtlest test of integrity is the desire to be liked.

Leaders, parents, even partners often sacrifice truth on the altar of acceptance. We soften our convictions to avoid conflict, shape-shift our opinions to please, or stay silent when conscience whispers, *Speak*.

Approval feels like safety, but it's counterfeit security.

When we anchor our identity in others' perception, we lose the freedom that integrity brings.

Integrity may not always make you popular, but it makes you peaceful. There's a deep rest that comes from knowing your inner compass hasn't been sold for applause.

The most trusted leaders aren't those who tell people what they want to hear, but those who tell them what they need to hear, with grace, but without distortion.

Pressure and the Gift of Refinement
Pressure doesn't always break integrity. Sometimes, it refines it.

Like gold tested in fire, character clarified under strain becomes purer, more resilient. You begin to understand what truly matters, and what's merely noise.

After enough storms, you stop fearing them. Because you realize that integrity, once proven, doesn't just survive pressure, it transforms it into credibility.

A leader who has stood firm in crisis carries a quiet authority. A parent who keeps promises in chaos teaches children what faithfulness looks like.

The test, in hindsight, becomes the testimony.

Self-Reflection

1. What's your current pressure test, the area where compromise whispers most persuasively?

2. When have you chosen integrity under stress, and what peace followed that choice?

3. How might honesty about your own limits strengthen, rather than weaken, your influence?

Habits that Matter

- **Name the Pressure:** Identify one recurring situation where you feel tempted to bend your values. Prepare a truthful response before it next arises.

- **Decompression Ritual:** After stressful days, write down one moment when you acted with integrity. Let gratitude replace self-doubt.

- **Courage in Communication:** Practise one act of truthful speech this week, gentle but direct, especially in a situation where silence feels safer.

- **Anchor Phrase:** Repeat a simple grounding line in moments of stress, "Peace comes from truth."

Wholeness, Not Perfection

Somewhere along the way, we confused integrity with flawlessness.

We imagined that to be a person of principle means never stumbling, never doubting, never losing composure. But that ideal is brittle and false. Real integrity is not about *perfection*, it's about *integration*.

To live with integrity is to live undivided, to bring all parts of yourself, even the imperfect ones, into honest alignment. It's to stop hiding behind the myth of control and to lead, love, and live from a center that refuses to fragment under pressure.

Perfection pretends. Integrity confesses.

The Courage to Be Seen

In leadership and in life, people follow honesty more than they follow flawlessness.

There's a quiet strength in saying, *I don't have all the answers.* There's wisdom in admitting, *I got that wrong.* Those words, though humbling, carry the power to restore trust faster than any defense ever could.

Years ago, I made a decision that backfired badly. It wasn't unethical, but it was unwise, an overreach of confidence. I spent weeks trying to fix the optics, to manage the story. But the more I tried to protect my image, the more exhausted I became.

Finally, in a meeting, I dropped the performance and said, "That was my mistake. I overestimated what we could handle, and you paid for it."

Silence filled the room, but it wasn't hostile. It was healing. People nodded. The air felt lighter. Integrity had done what ego couldn't, it had rebuilt trust through humility.

That moment taught me that transparency isn't weakness; it's leadership in its truest form. Because when you tell the truth about your flaws, you give everyone else permission to stop pretending too.

Integration vs. Image

In a world obsessed with image management, integrity calls us back to inner coherence.

Modern culture trains us to curate personas, professional, social, digital. We filter reality to appear competent and composed. But the more we polish the surface, the more our inner world frays.

Integration begins when we stop chasing consistency of *appearance* and start pursuing consistency of *essence*.

You can tell when someone lives from that place. Their words carry weight because they're grounded in congruence. They don't need to project confidence; they *are* confident, not because they're perfect, but because they're whole.

A leader who admits imperfection commands more respect than one who fakes certainty.

A parent who apologizes teaches more than one who pretends to be infallible.

Wholeness, not flawlessness, is what earns enduring trust.

The Mirror of Mistakes

Integrity isn't the absence of mistakes, it's the refusal to let mistakes define you.

Failure, handled truthfully, becomes the mirror that refines character.

When I reflect on the people I most admire, none of them are unblemished. They are those who have stumbled deeply yet emerged wiser, softer, and more grounded. Their integrity isn't untested, it's *tempered*.

A friend of mine, a senior leader, once told me that his turning point came after a public professional failure. "It was humiliating," he said. "But it forced me to confront the difference between my role and my identity. I realized I'd been building my worth on my performance, not my principles."

That insight freed him. He began leading more humanely, not from fear of falling, but from gratitude for growth.

Integrity matures when we stop hiding our scars and start honoring what they've taught us.

The Father's Grace

As a father, I've learned that integrity in parenting has little to do with being right and everything to do with being *real*.

Children don't need perfect parents; they need honest ones. They can handle our humanity, our frustrations, our flaws, our failures, as long as they know we are willing to own them.

There was a night when I lost my patience with my children over something trivial. Later, sitting in the dark, I felt the weight of it. So I went back, knelt beside them, and said, "I was wrong. I let my anger talk louder than my love."

Their forgiveness was instant, but more importantly, their eyes showed understanding. They learned that love and imperfection can coexist.

That moment taught me that integrity isn't the absence of error, it's the presence of grace after it.

And it's grace that transforms integrity from a rule into a relationship.

The Gift of Transparency

Transparency is the bridge between imperfection and integrity.

In leadership, transparency means telling the truth even when it's uncomfortable, especially when it's uncomfortable. It means saying, *Here's what we don't know yet. Here's what went wrong. Here's what we're learning.*

That level of candor doesn't diminish authority; it deepens it. Because people can't trust perfection, it's too brittle, too remote. They trust humanity.

I once led through a period of intense organizational change. People were anxious, rumors were swirling. Instead of issuing another polished memo, I gathered everyone and said plainly, "I don't have all the answers yet. Some of this will be messy. But here's what won't change, our commitment to each other, to our residents and to doing right."

The relief was visible. In uncertainty, truth became a stabilizer.

Transparency transforms fear into focus. It replaces speculation with honesty.

And it turns leadership from performance into partnership.

Grace Within Truth

Perfectionism is merciless. It sets impossible standards and punishes every shortfall. But integrity allows for grace, not as an excuse, but as an ecosystem where growth can flourish.

Grace within truth says: *You are accountable, but you are also redeemable.*

This is how families heal after conflict. It's how organizations recover after failure. It's how individuals learn to start again after moral missteps.

When we lead with integrity, we don't deny brokenness; we integrate it into wisdom.

Grace does not weaken truth, it completes it. It transforms moral rigidity into moral maturity.

A leader without grace becomes a judge. A leader with grace becomes a guide.

And that difference, between condemnation and restoration, determines whether integrity becomes a wall or a bridge.

The Long Work of Integration

Living an integrated life is slow work. It requires ongoing attention, daily reconciliation between your values and your behavior.

It means catching yourself in the small dissonances: the polite lie, the withheld apology, the temptation to posture. It means asking quietly, *Am I whole right now?*

Over time, that question becomes an inner compass. You begin to feel misalignment not as guilt, but as discomfort, a call back to integrity.

And the reward is peace. Not the fragile peace of perfectionism, but the deep calm of coherence, knowing you're the same person everywhere, even in private.

That wholeness is rare. It's magnetic. Because people are drawn not to those who never fall, but to those who fall honestly and rise humbly.

Self-Reflection

1. Where are you mistaking perfection for integrity in your own life or leadership?

2. How do you usually respond to your own mistakes, with judgment or with grace?

3. What might transparency look like in one relationship or role this week?

Habits that Matter

- **Daily Integration Check:** At the end of each day, ask, "Where did I live divided? Where did I live whole?"

- **Apology as Strength:** Practice one honest apology this week, quick, clean, without justification.

- **Grace Reflection:** Write a brief note to yourself about a past mistake, not to relive it, but to honor what it taught you.

- **Transparency Talk:** In your next meeting or family discussion, share one learning from failure instead of a success story.

The Quiet Currency of Trust

Trust is the quiet currency of all human connection.

It cannot be bought, demanded, or inherited. It must be earned, not once, but continually, through the steady accumulation of integrity over time.

In leadership, trust is what allows authority to function without coercion.
In family, it's what allows love to deepen without fear.

Integrity is the mint where this currency is forged. Every word kept, every truth spoken, every consistent act, they're all deposits into an account that, once full, can weather storms without collapsing.

The Slow Build

Trust rarely forms in grand gestures. It grows like a slow dawn, imperceptible at first, but steady, dependable, inevitable.

People learn to trust not because of what you *say*, but because of what you *repeat*.

When you keep showing up.
When your tone matches your message.
When your promises survive inconvenience.

Over time, consistency becomes credibility.

I once worked with a leader who was not the most charismatic in the room. His presentations were plain, his manner gentle. But when he spoke, people listened. They trusted him, because he never said anything he didn't mean. His word was simple, and sacred.

That's the paradox of integrity: it's quiet, but it echoes. Its influence doesn't shout; it accumulates.

Trust, like sediment, builds layer by layer, and once formed, it becomes the bedrock on which everything else stands.

The Fragility of the Account
If trust is a bank account, then integrity is the interest rate. Every act of honesty compounds; every compromise withdraws.

And the cruel truth is that withdrawals are instant, while deposits take time.

A single lie can erase months of truth-telling. A single betrayal can undo years of reliability. That's why integrity is not only a moral choice, it's a strategic one.

In leadership, credibility is your most valuable currency. You can't lead people who doubt your word. You can't inspire them if they suspect your motives.

The same is true in family life. Children who grow up in unpredictable households, where promises are made and forgotten, emotions swing without warning, learn early that safety can't be trusted. And that insecurity follows them into adulthood.

Rebuilding trust, then, is not about apology alone, it's about predictability. It's about proving, through repetition, that what broke once can hold again.

Truth as Tender
Truth is the purest tender in the economy of trust.

It's tempting to think that people want reassurance, but what they actually crave is reality. Even painful truth is better than comforting deceit.

I've seen leaders destroy credibility not through wrongdoing, but through spin, through sugar-coating the facts, delaying candor,

pretending control when chaos ruled.
They meant well, but the omission felt like betrayal.

When people sense that you're withholding the truth, they fill the silence with fear. But when you tell the truth, cleanly, promptly, even when it stings, they feel safe, because they know where they stand.

Truth doesn't erode loyalty; it refines it.

In the home, this principle is just as vital. Children learn emotional trust when parents speak honestly, not in cruelty, but in clarity. "Dad's upset," "Mum's tired," "We're figuring this out", those small admissions build stability. They prove that truth can be handled without panic.

To tell the truth, even gently, is to say: *You can trust me with reality.*

The Humility Dividend
Integrity and humility are inseparable. Without humility, integrity becomes pride disguised as virtue, a performance of morality instead of a posture of sincerity.

Humility acknowledges that we are all capable of falling short, that trust, even when earned, must be guarded vigilantly.

A leader once said to me, "Every day I assume trust is on probation."

It wasn't cynicism; it was stewardship. He understood that leadership isn't ownership, it's a lease, renewed daily through behavior.

Humility turns integrity from self-righteousness into service. It says: *I don't demand your trust; I intend to deserve it.*

And that mindset transforms culture. People stop fearing accountability because it's no longer about proving worth, it's about protecting relationship.

The humble leader admits, "I'm learning." The humble parent says, "I overreacted." Those moments don't diminish authority; they humanize it.

When humility meets integrity, trust becomes unshakeable, not because it's perfect, but because it's real.

Consistency as Credibility
Inconsistency is the enemy of trust. People can handle your flaws, they can't handle your unpredictability.

The mind needs patterns to feel safe. When your responses vary wildly, when your moods dictate your tone, when your commitments fluctuate with convenience, people withdraw, not because they dislike you, but because they can't locate you.

Consistency doesn't mean monotony. It means reliability of principle, that people know what to expect from your character, even if your circumstances change.

One of the most stabilizing forces in both leadership and family life is emotional consistency. Calm under pressure, fairness in frustration, honesty in confusion, these steady patterns signal safety.

When integrity and consistency align, people begin to relax around you.

And relaxation is the soil of creativity, connection, and love.

The Long Arc of Trust
The beautiful thing about trust is that it compounds invisibly. At first, it's fragile, like glass. But over years of consistent honesty,

it becomes like tempered steel, flexible, resilient, and quietly strong.

People who have trusted you once will trust you faster the next time. That's moral capital, not the transactional kind measured in reputation, but the relational kind measured in faith.

I've watched leaders carry teams through crises simply because of the reserves they'd built in better seasons. When mistakes happened, forgiveness came swiftly, because trust had been stockpiled in advance.

Families operate the same way. A child who has known years of honesty will forgive a parent's mistake more readily. A spouse who's experienced steady truth will absorb the bumps of imperfection with grace.

Integrity stores trust like sunlight, it powers the dark seasons later.

When Trust Breaks
But what happens when it fails? Because even the most honest hearts falter.

When trust is broken, the temptation is to rush to repair, to demand forgiveness, to restore what's lost. But trust cannot be rebuilt in a hurry; it must be *re-earned, slowly, humbly, consistently.*

Apology is the beginning. Accountability is the bridge. Consistency is the proof.

I've seen broken trust restored, but only when remorse was matched by reliability.

One father, a friend, after an affair told me, "I thought saying sorry would be enough. It wasn't. It was every day of showing up, doing the right thing quietly, for as long as it took."

He rebuilt trust brick by brick, not by promising perfection, but by demonstrating integrity.

That's the paradox of trust: though fragile, it is also renewable, if humility holds steady and truth never wavers.

The Invisible Wealth

When trust becomes part of your identity, it changes how you move through the world. You speak more carefully. You act more thoughtfully. You lead more humanely.

Because you know that every interaction, no matter how small, either strengthens or weakens that invisible bond.

Integrity builds wealth that no market can measure: the wealth of credibility, peace, and respect.

People follow trustworthy leaders not because they must, but because they *want to*. They stay not out of fear, but out of faith.

And those who live with that kind of moral capital, at home or at work, leave behind something rarer than success: they leave behind *security*.

The knowledge that someone like you existed, steady, truthful, whole, becomes an inheritance others can build upon.

Self-Reflection

1. Where in your life are you making daily deposits into the account of trust?

2. Have you made any quiet withdrawals lately, through inconsistency, omission, or impatience?

3. What does humility look like in your relationships right now?

Habits that Matter

- **Trust Ledger:** Choose one key relationship (team, partner, or child). Note one behavior that strengthens trust and one that erodes it. Focus on the strengthening action for a week.

- **Truth Audit:** Review your last few difficult conversations. Did you protect truth or comfort? Practice truth with gentleness next time.

- **Consistency Habit:** Identify a small ritual of reliability, a weekly message, check-in, or family moment, and make it sacred.

- **Forgiveness Practice:** If trust has been broken, start with one honest action today, not a promise, but a pattern.

Becoming the Same Person Everywhere

There's a rare kind of peace that comes when you stop shape-shifting, when you no longer need one voice for the boardroom, another for home, and another in the quiet of your own mind. That peace is the fruit of integrity fully matured: becoming the same person everywhere.

It's the freedom of moral congruence, the alignment between belief, behavior, and belonging. It's when your inner world and outer world finally tell the same story.

To live that way is not easy in a world that rewards adaptation over authenticity. But it's the only way to remain whole.

The Multiplicity of Masks
Most people live with subtle fragmentation. We wear masks suited to context: the confident leader, the agreeable colleague, the calm parent, the composed friend.
Each role has expectations, and somewhere in the performance, the real self begins to fade.

I know this because I lived it.

For years, I carried two selves, the professional me, polished and articulate, and the private me, thoughtful but often tired, craving honesty. I justified the split as necessity. "This is what leadership demands," I told myself. "They need strength, not honesty."

But duplicity, even well-intentioned, drains the soul. You begin to lose the quiet joy of authenticity. You start calculating responses instead of offering truth. You start performing warmth instead of living it.

Then one day, you look in the mirror and realize the reflection no longer feels like you.

That's when the work of wholeness begins, the slow and deliberate merging of all the selves you've scattered along the way.

Authenticity as Discipline
Authenticity is not impulse. It's not blurting out every emotion or opinion. It's disciplined transparency, the courage to be truthful without losing grace.

It means speaking honestly while staying kind, holding conviction while staying humble, showing vulnerability without demanding sympathy.

A leader once told me, "I'm tired of pretending. I want to show up as myself." I said, "Then start by defining who that self is, and live him everywhere."

He did. He began small, by aligning how he spoke privately with how he spoke publicly, by ending the quiet exaggerations meant to impress, by replacing "image management" with quiet truth.

The transformation was remarkable. People didn't lose respect, they gained it. He became trustworthy because he became *consistent*.

Authenticity is not raw exposure; it's integrated honesty. It's choosing to live undivided.

The Mirror of Leadership and Home
There's no clearer mirror for authenticity than the home.

You can't fake presence there. You can't curate your tone for effect. Your family sees the version of you that colleagues never meet, the impatient one, the distracted one, the silent one.

And yet, the truest test of integrity is not how you perform in the spotlight, but how you love in the shadows.

A leader who is admired publicly but resented privately hasn't succeeded; he's simply compartmentalized.

I've learned that the more integrated my life becomes, the easier it is to lead with peace. When I am consistent at home, listening well, speaking gently, staying honest, those habits follow me into work.

And when I practice patience in the workplace, with colleagues, with decisions, with results, that patience comes home with me too.

Wholeness works both ways.

When you become the same person everywhere, you stop carrying the burden of performance. You don't have to switch personas; you simply *are*.

That freedom radiates calm. People sense when you're not divided inside. They trust it instinctively, because consistency feels safe, and safety breeds loyalty.

The Freedom of Wholeness
The greatest gift integrity gives is freedom, the kind that no title, success, or recognition can match.

Freedom from pretending.
Freedom from overexplaining.
Freedom from the exhausting treadmill of approval.

When your life becomes one continuous narrative, you no longer have to edit yourself for each chapter. You no longer seek validation from external applause because your sense of worth is internally settled.

It's not arrogance; it's peace.

The French writer Albert Camus once said, *"Integrity has no need of rules."* He didn't mean that integrity dismisses structure, but that when you're truly aligned within yourself, you no longer need to check every decision against a code, because your conscience *is* the code.

Wholeness makes morality instinctive. You act truthfully not out of duty, but out of identity.

That's why the most grounded leaders often seem effortless. Their decisions flow naturally from who they are, not from calculation. Their yes means yes, their no means no, and in a world full of spin, that simplicity feels revolutionary.

When Authenticity Costs
Of course, being the same person everywhere carries risk. Authenticity has a price.

When you choose congruence, you will sometimes disappoint people who preferred your mask. You will lose comfort, and occasionally, you will lose company.

But you will gain peace, the kind that can't be replicated through applause.

I once had to make a choice between pleasing a powerful partner and honoring a principle I believed in. The cost was real, opportunity lost, reputation questioned. But in the quiet afterward, I slept better than I had in months.

Integrity doesn't always make life easier. It makes it lighter.

When you're no longer torn between versions of yourself, every step feels steadier, even on uncertain ground.

Wholeness as Legacy

The most enduring legacies are not achievements, but consistencies.

People remember steady hearts, not perfect résumés. They remember how you made them feel safe to be themselves, because you were brave enough to be yourself.

That's the paradox of wholeness: it's deeply personal, but its impact is profoundly communal. Your authenticity gives others permission to shed pretense too. Your congruence becomes contagious.

When a leader lives the same truth at every level, boardroom, backroom, living room, backyard, integrity becomes culture. When a father keeps his tone, whether with his child or his colleague, love becomes lineage.

That is how character multiplies. That is how legacy is written, not in accolades, but in atmosphere.

Integration as a Lifelong Journey

Becoming the same person everywhere isn't a destination. It's a rhythm, daily, imperfect, but intentional.

It means catching yourself when you begin to drift toward duality. It means apologizing quickly when you've said something that didn't sound like your truest self. It means resisting the urge to impress and choosing instead to express.

And it means keeping your private world large enough to sustain your public one. Because the larger the stage, the deeper the roots must go.

A life of integrity is not about shining brighter; it's about shining true.

The Final Integration

One day, when all the titles fade and the applause dies down, the only question that will matter is: *Was I the same person everywhere?*

Did the version of me my children knew match the one my team saw?
Did my inner motives align with my outer words?
Did I live with coherence, even when it cost comfort?

If the answer, even imperfectly, is yes, then you have lived with integrity. You have stayed whole in a world that fragments easily.

And that wholeness, quiet and steadfast, becomes your greatest legacy.

Self-Reflection

1. In what areas of life do you feel divided between personas?

2. What would it look like to merge those selves into one coherent story?

3. Who in your life models that kind of integrated authenticity, and what can you learn from them?

Habits that Matter

- **Persona Inventory:** List the different "versions" of yourself you tend to show in different settings. What value drives each one? What would it look like to unify them?

- **Congruence Check:** Before each major decision, ask, "Will this choice make me more or less whole?"

- **Authentic Speech:** In your next difficult conversation, replace careful performance with plain honesty.

- **Role Reflection:** At the end of the week, journal on this question: "Did I live as one person, everywhere?"

Closing Thought

Integrity ends where it began, not with rules, but with presence.

The courage to be whole.
The humility to be honest.
The grace to be the same person, everywhere.

Integrity is the stabilizing force of the FatherFrame™, the alignment that keeps leadership whole, trustworthy, and anchored in purpose.

Because when you live that way, consistently, quietly, truthfully, your life itself becomes a kind of leadership. Not through speeches or strategy, but through the unmistakable power of being real.

And that is how wholeness becomes legacy.

Integrity turns leadership inward, asking who you are. Service turns it outward, asking who you're here for. When your inner life becomes steady and honest, the natural next step is to use that wholeness for the good of others.

People follow leaders who serve, not leaders who shine. The next chapter explores the kind of leadership that lifts, supports, and releases, the leadership that sees its power as responsibility, not privilege.

Chapter Seven — Service: Leadership Beyond Self

"The most influential leaders are those who turn outward, measuring success not by what they gain, but by how others grow because of them."

Service shifts leadership from self-preservation to people-elevation. When leaders adopt a posture of service, they stop asking "What do I need?" and start asking "What do others need from me to thrive?"

This chapter explores how the heart of fatherhood, giving, guiding, and supporting, becomes the heart of enduring leadership. Service dismantles ego, rebuilds relationships, and fosters cultures where people feel empowered rather than controlled. True influence is not found in authority; it is earned in the daily, deliberate choice to put others first.

Service expands the FatherFrame™ by turning leadership from self-focused performance into others-focused contribution. When we view leadership as giving rather than gaining, influence grows without force. This chapter unpacks the power of serving in ways that elevate the people and environments we lead.

The Turning Outward

The greatest transformation in any leader's life happens at the moment they stop asking, *How far can I go?* and start asking, *How far can I take others?*

That shift, from ambition to service, marks the true crossing from authority to leadership. It's the turning outward, when ego yields to empathy, and success finds its fulfilment in significance.

For years, I measured my growth by metrics: revenue, promotions, projects completed, applause earned. Each milestone felt like proof that I was moving forward, until I realized I was mostly moving *alone*.

Then one day, something shifted. A member of my team presented her first major proposal to the Executive. I watched from the back of the room as she spoke with quiet confidence, her work shining. When the presentation ended, she turned, found my eyes, and smiled, not in thanks, but in shared joy.

In that moment, I felt a strange mix of pride and humility. It dawned on me that leadership's truest reward isn't personal advancement; it's seeing others rise on the shoulders of your influence.

The Evolution from Self to Service

Every meaningful leader must outgrow the gravitational pull of self-interest.

Ambition is not wrong, it's the engine that gets us moving. But if it never evolves into purpose, it becomes consumption.

The corporate world often idolizes the self-made success story: the visionary, the disrupter, the name on the building. But history remembers a different kind of greatness, those who used their success as scaffolding for others.

Service doesn't mean surrendering your ambition; it means sanctifying it. It's about directing your strength toward the flourishing of others.

When a leader's energy shifts from accumulation to multiplication, everything changes, meetings gain meaning, metrics gain soul, and influence gains permanence.

The Father's Example
Parenting taught me what leadership books or university could not: that love becomes real only when it costs you something.

No father wakes at 2 a.m. to feed a child because it's efficient. He does it because the well-being of another has become inseparable from his own.

Leadership at its best mirrors that kind of service, not transactional, not strategic, but relational. It's the instinct to protect, nurture, and develop the people entrusted to your care.

There's a quiet dignity in the father who chooses the back row at the school concert so others can see, or the leader who gives credit to the team when things go right and takes responsibility when they go wrong.

Both know the same truth: that love and leadership are verbs, not positions.

Service as Strength
Service is not weakness; it's power restrained for the sake of others.

It's what philosopher Henri Nouwen called "downward mobility", the movement from status to solidarity. It's choosing to influence through example rather than authority.

In the modern workplace, that might look like a CEO who visits the warehouse floor before making a logistics decision, or a manager who spends a day doing the tasks they once delegated.

That kind of proximity builds credibility. When people know you understand their world, they open theirs to you.

And in family life, service looks even simpler, staying up late to help with homework, cooking dinner when you're exhausted, sitting in silence beside someone who's hurting.

Service rarely makes headlines, but it makes households and organizations whole.

The Mirror of Motive

Of course, service can also disguise ambition. It's easy to perform humility for recognition. The hardest kind of service is the kind that remains unseen, the help that receives no applause.

I once asked a team member why she volunteered for the least visible projects. She smiled and said, "Because they still matter."

That sentence struck me deeply.
True service doesn't need a spotlight; it carries its own illumination.

Integrity gives service its purity. You serve not to be seen, but because it's who you are.

The paradox is that when you stop chasing recognition, your influence expands. People trust those who help without agenda. They sense the authenticity of it.

Service, when unforced, becomes contagious.

The Shift from Achievement to Legacy

The older I get, the more I believe that legacy is not what we build but who we build.

Buildings crumble, programs fade, strategies evolve. But people, people carry your impact forward.

The world may never remember the projects I led, but it might remember the people I encouraged. It might remember the quiet mornings when I listened instead of instructing, or the moments when I gave someone else the stage.

Those aren't small acts. They're seeds, and service is the soil where those seeds take root.

A good leader achieves success.
A great leader multiplies it.

Self-Reflection

1. Who has benefited most from your leadership so far, and how intentionally have you served their growth?

2. When was the last time you felt joy in someone else's success as if it were your own?

3. Where might your strength be better used to lift rather than to lead?

Habits that Matter

- **Inversion Exercise:** This week, spend one day viewing your role purely through the lens of those you serve. Ask, "How can I make their work easier?"

- **Silent Help:** Do one generous act that no one knows about, and never mention it again.

- **Legacy Mapping:** List three people whose futures you can tangibly improve. Schedule one conversation or action to invest in each.

- **Family Service Ritual:** Choose one weekly household task to take off someone else's plate, not as duty, but as devotion.

The Paradox of Power

Power is one of the most misunderstood words in leadership. We often treat it as a resource to acquire, a weapon to wield, or a prize to protect. Yet the paradox of power is this: the more tightly you hold it, the less real it becomes.

True power, the kind that transforms rather than controls, is never taken; it's entrusted. It flows not from dominance but from *stewardship*, not from status but from service.

Power doesn't reveal character; it amplifies it. Whatever is within you, humility or pride, integrity or insecurity, will echo louder once authority hands you a microphone.

Authority vs. Influence

Authority is positional. It can be given by a title, a role, or a structure. Influence, however, is relational, it's given by people who have chosen to trust you.

The world runs on authority, but it *moves* on influence.

A father may have authority over his children by law, but he only has influence if they believe in his love. A CEO may have authority by title, but their words only inspire if their people sense alignment between intention and action.

Power that demands obedience creates compliance. Power that earns respect creates commitment.

And the difference is stewardship.

Stewardship asks, *What has been placed in my care, and how can I use it for others' good?*

Dominance says, *What can I control to protect myself?*

The first multiplies. The second drains.

The Ego's Illusion

Ego is a master illusionist. It convinces you that control is safety, that applause is affirmation, that authority must be displayed to be real.

But the most secure leaders are often the quietest. They don't need to assert power because their presence already commands trust.

The insecure leader, by contrast, exhausts themselves in performance, speaking over others, micromanaging, competing for credit. It looks strong but feels desperate.

When I first entered senior leadership, I mistook decisiveness for dominance. I believed clarity required control. It took years, and a few mistakes, to realize that the loudest person in the room isn't always leading; sometimes they're just *shielding*.

The ego-driven leader hoards power. The servant leader shares it.

And paradoxically, in sharing it, they gain more.

Stewardship as Strength

Stewardship reframes power as responsibility. It understands that authority is not ownership, it's a trust.

Every decision a leader makes affects lives beyond their own. Every word spoken from authority has moral weight.

The best leaders know this and handle power like something fragile. They measure before they move, and they listen before they act.

There's a story I love about a hospital CEO who, instead of starting each week in the boardroom, began in the emergency department. He'd walk the wards, talk with nurses, ask what was broken, not metaphorically, but literally: "What's not working today?"

He didn't lose authority by doing that; he multiplied it. Because stewardship dignifies others. It turns power from a pyramid into a circle.

The Leader's Shadow
Every leader casts a shadow, the emotional climate created by their presence.

If your power is rooted in fear, your shadow is cold and long. If it's rooted in service, your shadow is shade, a place of safety.

When I think of the best leaders I've known, they were steady. Not loud, not flamboyant, steady. Their steadiness didn't come from apathy, but from alignment. They had nothing to prove, so their energy could be spent proving others instead.

Their confidence wasn't volume; it was gravity.

That's the paradox: people follow servant leaders not because they command, but because they *anchor*.

The Father's Lesson in Power
Fatherhood is the quietest training ground for stewardship.

Children misread power at first, they think it's about control, about who can decide bedtime or hold the keys. But as they grow, they come to see the deeper truth: the parent's power was never to dominate but to *protect*.

My own children taught me that restraint is a higher form of strength. When anger flares, it takes power to stay calm. When authority could coerce, it takes more power to persuade through love.

The most powerful thing a father can do is use his strength gently.

And the same is true for leadership. The measure of maturity is how much restraint you can apply to the authority you hold.

Emptying thy Self

There's an ancient wisdom, echoed in philosophy, faith, and psychology alike, that says fullness begins with emptying.

To lead from the soul, you must let go of the illusion that leadership is about you.

Ego asks, *How am I doing?*
Service asks, *How are they doing because of me?*

That one shift transforms the entire architecture of power. You stop performing and start parenting, not in a paternalistic sense, but in a deeply human one: caring for others' growth more than your own glory.

And the paradox deepens, the more you empty yourself of ego, the more you are filled with purpose. The less you strive to control, the more your influence expands.

Because people don't follow titles, they follow peace.

The Moral Weight of Power

The philosopher Lao Tzu said, *"The best leaders are those the people barely know exist."*

That isn't invisibility; it's humility so radiant that it doesn't need to announce itself.

Power used well is invisible. It serves without spectacle. It builds without branding.

But when power is abused, through manipulation, exploitation, or indifference, it leaves a long scar. History's most devastating failures were not born of incompetence, but of arrogance.

Leadership is sacred because it touches human souls. Power, when misused, corrodes trust. But when used humbly, it redeems it.

To steward power well, you must see it as temporary, something loaned, not owned.

When to Step Back

Sometimes, the greatest act of leadership is stepping aside.

The ego hates this. It equates succession with obsolescence. But the servant leader knows that letting others shine is not losing influence; it's multiplying it.

I once had a mentor who, after decades of leading, began declining invitations to speak. "I've had my say," he told me. "It's their turn now."

There was no bitterness in his tone, only peace. He understood what few do: that the truest mark of power is how gently you let it go.

Self-Reflection

1. How do you define power, control, influence, or stewardship?

2. When was the last time you used your authority to elevate someone else?

3. Where might restraint, rather than assertion, serve your leadership more deeply?

Habits that Matter

- **Power Audit:** List your spheres of influence, home, team, community. For each, note one way you could share authority more intentionally.

- **Listening Leadership:** In your next meeting, speak last. Let others shape the conversation before you do.

- **Restraint Practice:** Notice one moment this week where your instinct is to control. Pause. Choose to trust instead.

- **Empowerment Act:** Delegate a meaningful decision to someone younger or less experienced, not as tokenism, but as trust.

The Servant's Posture

Humility is not a natural reflex in leadership.

From our earliest years, we are taught to stand tall, to project confidence, to be noticed.

But the great paradox of leadership, and of life, is that true greatness begins with lowering oneself.

Humility is not humiliation. It is the quiet strength of groundedness, the ability to stand firm without standing *over* others. It is posture, not personality: the physical and spiritual alignment that reminds you that every person you lead is not beneath you, but beside you.

The Posture of Perspective
Everything in leadership begins with where you stand, and how you see.

Perspective is posture in motion. When a leader looks down on people, they see subordinates. When they stand among people, they see partners. And when they kneel, figuratively or literally, they see what power was always meant to serve: humanity.

I once visited a logistics warehouse where the general manager was walking the floor. He didn't stride through with a clipboard or entourage. He bent down to pick up a loose label, greeted a packer by name, and asked her about her son's soccer finals.

It wasn't a performance. It was posture, attentive, present, unpretentious.

The effect was remarkable. Everyone on that floor worked harder, smiled wider. He wasn't managing; he was *ministering*.

That's what humility does: it recalibrates presence. It reminds people that leadership isn't about distance; it's about proximity.

The Father's Posture

Fatherhood has a way of teaching humility, sometimes gently, often abruptly.

The first time you hold a newborn, the world rearranges itself. You realize you are not the center anymore. The child doesn't care about your title, your credentials, or your schedule. They care only that you're there.

That moment of holding, fragile, sacred, grounding, becomes the truest metaphor for leadership: power placed in service of something smaller, yet infinitely more precious.

As children grow, humility shifts shape. It's no longer about protection alone; it's about patience. The humility to listen to questions you don't have answers for. The humility to let them fail without rescuing too soon. The humility to admit, "I don't know, but I'm learning with you."

Every father learns that love has a posture, and it's not the raised voice or the pointed finger. It's the open hand.

Leadership, too, has an open-hand posture, one that gives freedom instead of fear, dignity instead of dominance.

The Myth of the Strong Leader

For too long, leadership models have equated humility with weakness, as though empathy dilutes authority. The myth of the "strong leader" still pervades boardrooms and institutions: the decisive voice, the unflinching stance, the unyielding will.

But strength without humility becomes tyranny. It breeds distance and fear.

The strongest leaders are those who can kneel without losing authority, who can say, "I need your help," without losing respect.

Jim Collins, in *Good to Great*, called this the "Level 5 Leader", someone who combines fierce resolve with personal humility. It's a rare blend, but unmistakable when you see it.

These are the leaders who deflect credit, absorb blame, and never confuse position with worth. They know that humility is not self-deprecation; it's self-definition, knowing who you are so clearly that you no longer need to prove it.

The Practice of Presence
Humility shows itself most in how we inhabit moments.

A humble leader listens longer than they speak. They make space for silence, for reflection, for another's story. They resist the impulse to fix before understanding.

I remember a leadership retreat where a senior executive shared how his company had gone through a crisis. "I spent months trying to solve it," he said, "until one of our factory workers said, 'You've been listening to the problem, but not to the people living it.'"

That one sentence changed everything. He restructured his leadership rhythm around presence, not meetings, but conversations; not updates, but understanding.

And slowly, the culture healed.

Humility is the discipline of presence, showing up not to impress, but to *understand.*

The Weight of the Knee
Kneeling has long symbolized reverence, surrender, or service. But in leadership, it means something even subtler: the willingness to lower yourself to elevate someone else.

I saw this once in a young manager who, after a difficult presentation by a nervous team member, took a moment to walk over afterward. Instead of critique, he offered quiet praise and asked, "What did you learn about yourself today?"

It wasn't flattery, it was formation. He had chosen to kneel, metaphorically, to meet that person where they were instead of towering over them with authority.

In that exchange, humility became a form of teaching, one that reshaped confidence without breaking spirit.

Leadership posture isn't about physical height; it's about moral balance. Those who learn to bend their ego can carry far greater weight.

The Leader's Reflection
Humility is not an act you perform; it's a mirror you polish daily. Every time you resist defensiveness, every time you listen before judging, every time you choose empathy over efficiency, you polish that mirror.

Because when you kneel in leadership, you're not just lifting others; you're lifting the reflection of your truest self.

The servant's posture is not submission to people, it's submission to purpose. It's recognizing that leadership is not ownership, but stewardship; not elevation, but alignment.

When you approach your work, your relationships, and your influence from that low and steady posture, something extraordinary happens: people stop following you out of obligation and start following you out of trust.

And that trust, once born, carries farther than authority ever could.

Self-Reflection

1. Where does pride most easily disguise itself in your leadership, in expertise, position, or performance?

2. What would it look like to lower yourself this week, not in shame, but in service?

3. Who around you could rise higher if you shifted your posture from command to care?

Habits that Matter

- **The Listening Posture:** In your next meeting or conversation, consciously listen without interrupting for two full minutes. Notice how the dynamic shifts.

- **The Gratitude Bow:** At the end of each day, identify one person who made your work possible. Acknowledge them privately or publicly.

- **Perspective Walk:** Spend time in the workspace or environment of someone you lead. Observe what they see daily.

- **Quiet Servanthood:** Perform one act of help this week that no one expects, and expect no thanks in return.

The Economics of Giving

Every system, corporate, familial, or social, runs on an invisible economy.

It trades not only in money or resources but in trust, attention, and time.

And in that economy, generosity is the most undervalued currency.

Leadership that gives freely, of time, of trust, of credit, creates a culture of abundance.

Leadership that hoards these things creates scarcity, even in environments full of wealth.

The paradox is simple but profound:
When you give, you multiply. When you withhold, you diminish.

The Generous Mindset

Generosity is not about resources; it's about perspective.

It begins when you stop asking, *What do I get?* and start asking, *What can I contribute?*

A generous leader operates from the assumption that there is *enough*, enough credit to share, enough opportunity to go around, enough time to listen, enough kindness to give without running dry.

This mindset transforms culture. Teams that feel trusted take risks. Families that feel valued thrive. People who are given credit learn to give it back.

I once worked under a leader who, at the end of every major success, would say to the team, "I didn't do this, you did." It wasn't false modesty; it was accurate accounting.

He recognized that leadership isn't measured by how much you accumulate, but by how much you *circulate*.

The best leaders see success not as possession, but as flow.

The Currency of Time
The most generous thing a leader can give is attention.

Time is the one resource no one can replenish, and yet it's the one we squander most easily.

In a world obsessed with productivity, giving your time, undivided and unhurried, is an act of profound generosity.

I once met a CEO who scheduled thirty minutes every morning simply to walk the floor and talk to people, not about metrics, but about meaning. "It's inefficient," he laughed, "but it's where the truth lives."

He understood what many forget: efficiency builds output; generosity builds loyalty.

The same holds true at home. I've learned that my children don't remember the days I bought them something; they remember the days I *sat still*, really listening, fully present, no phone, no agenda.

Leadership, whether corporate or parental, always begins with time. Because giving time tells people: *You matter more than my schedule.*

The Currency of Trust
Trust is another form of giving, and one of the most courageous.

When you trust someone, you hand them a piece of your influence. You take a risk on their potential. You say, *I believe in you, even before the proof.*

That's not naïveté; that's investment.

In economics, trust functions like liquidity, it keeps the system flowing. Without it, every interaction becomes transactional, cautious, and slow.

When leaders hoard trust, insisting on control, they create bottlenecks. When they distribute it freely, they create innovation.

One of my mentors used to delegate whole projects to emerging leaders with minimal oversight. "They'll make mistakes," he'd say. "But they'll grow faster than if I protect them."

And they did. Because trust, given before it's fully earned, tends to produce the very competence it anticipates.

At home, this principle is even more delicate. Letting children make decisions, even small ones, communicates belief. It tells them, *I see the adult you're becoming.* And nothing shapes confidence more than being trusted.

The Currency of Credit
Few things reveal the character of a leader like how they handle recognition.

Small-minded leaders hoard credit like currency, rationing it out to protect their image. Great leaders scatter it freely, knowing it costs them nothing but earns them everything.

When you give credit away, you build credibility. When you take credit you didn't earn, you lose both.

There's a subtle power in public gratitude. A thank-you in a meeting, a name mentioned in an email, a story shared upward about someone's contribution, these small gestures of generosity are leadership gold.

They communicate, *I see you. I value you. You're part of this.*

It's astonishing how loyalty deepens when people feel seen. They'll work harder not because they're told to, but because they're trusted to.

The same is true in families. A spouse or child who feels appreciated doesn't demand perfection; they reciprocate love. Generosity multiplies not by force, but by example.

The Myth of Scarcity
Many leaders operate from a scarcity mindset, the fear that giving diminishes them.

They believe time given is time lost, trust given is risk increased, credit given is status reduced.

But the opposite is true.

Scarcity isolates. Generosity connects.

When you lead with generosity, you create psychological safety, that sense of *enoughness* that allows others to experiment, to speak up, to create.

Scarcity says, *There's only room for one winner.*
Generosity says, *There's room for everyone to grow.*

In economic terms, generosity changes the multiplier effect. Every act of giving, time, trust, encouragement, produces a ripple that exceeds the cost.

I've seen it in workplaces and homes alike.
When a leader shares credit, morale lifts across the room. When a father praises his child's effort instead of the outcome, confidence grows beyond that moment.

Generosity makes people bigger. Scarcity makes them smaller.

Giving as Strategy

Generosity is not soft, it's strategic. It builds cultures that outperform because they are emotionally rich.

A generous organization attracts loyalty; a stingy one breeds turnover.
A generous home nurtures resilience; a critical one breeds fear.

When you give freely, when you mentor, teach, listen, and affirm, you create self-reinforcing cycles of growth. The people you invest in begin investing in others.

It's the most sustainable form of influence.

When I think of the best leaders I've known, they all share one common trait: they left people richer than they found them, not financially, but emotionally, intellectually, spiritually.

They understood that the purpose of power is to circulate goodness, not consolidate control.

Self-Reflection

1. Where in your leadership do you default to scarcity, fearing that giving will leave you empty?

2. What would generosity look like in your use of time, attention, or recognition this week?

3. Who could benefit most from being trusted before they've proven themselves?

Habits that Matter

- **The Generosity Audit:** At the end of each day, list three things you gave, time, praise, or help, and three opportunities you missed. Reflect on what held you back.

- **Trust Dividend:** Delegate one meaningful decision to someone untested. Support quietly and observe how they grow.

- **Credit Transfer:** Publicly recognize someone's effort in front of their peers. Make it specific, sincere, and unexpected.

- **Time Investment:** Block one uninterrupted hour each week solely to listen, to a team member, a partner, or a child. Guard it as sacred.

A Life Poured Out

There comes a point in every leader's life, and in every parent's, when you realize that the measure of success is no longer what you've built, but what you've *given away*.

Service, when practiced long enough, becomes less of an act and more of an identity. It reshapes the heart until giving feels as natural as breathing, until generosity ceases to be something you *do* and becomes who you *are*.

A life poured out is not one depleted; it's one fulfilled.

The paradox is this: the more you give of yourself, time, energy, wisdom, forgiveness, compassion, the more you discover there is to give. Service multiplies the soul.

The Overflow Principle

We often think of service as subtraction, that every act of giving costs us something finite. But life has its own kind of economy, and it doesn't run on arithmetic. It runs on overflow.

When your giving flows from love rather than obligation, you don't run out, you fill up.

I saw this most clearly in my father. He never lectured on generosity; he simply lived it. He'd stop to help neighbors, fix broken things that weren't his, and listen to people long after others had turned away. I used to wonder where he found the energy.

Now I know: he didn't *find* it; he *created* it. Generosity was his renewal. Service was his rest.

The more he gave, the more grounded he seemed, as though pouring himself out kept his spirit clear of the sediment that selfishness leaves behind.

And I've come to believe that's true for all of us.

Service, at its deepest, is not depletion. It's circulation.

The Legacy of Quiet Servants

The most enduring legacies are not carved in stone or recorded in balance sheets; they're etched into people.

I once attended the retirement celebration of a Man who had worked nearly forty years in Aged Care. He was not famous. His title had never been grand. But the room that night overflowed, hundreds of people, young and old, who stood to tell stories of how he had changed their lives.

Some spoke of how he'd found them care when they had none, others of how he'd mentored them into careers, and still others simply of how he'd *listened*.

When he stood to speak, he said only this: "I didn't plan a legacy. I just tried to be useful."

There was no strategy behind his influence, only consistency of compassion.

That's the quiet truth of service: it doesn't announce itself. It simply shows up, day after day, until one day the sum of all those small acts becomes a story that outlives you.

The Weight of Emptiness

To pour yourself out is to live counter to the culture of accumulation.

The world tells us to keep filling, our calendars, our homes, our egos, as though fullness equals life. But fullness without flow turns stagnant.

When you pour yourself out in service, you make room for renewal. You discover that space, the emptiness left behind, is not loss but invitation.

I once spent a season of burnout where I'd been giving without grounding. I thought I was serving, but in truth, I was striving, doing for others what I hadn't first anchored within myself.

Service that forgets self-care becomes sacrifice without meaning.

The paradox is that the most sustainable giving comes not from depletion but from wholeness. You pour from a full cup, not an empty one.

So the discipline of a life poured out includes the humility to rest, to receive, to be restored. Because even rivers need replenishment.

A leader who never allows themselves to be refilled eventually gives bitterness instead of blessing.

The Father's Legacy
Fatherhood taught me that pouring yourself out doesn't weaken love, it expands it.

There's a peculiar tenderness in watching your children grow into independence, in realizing that the hours, the sacrifices, the sleepless nights, have all culminated in their ability to stand without you.

It's both loss and victory, the quiet ache of completion.

I remember walking with my eldest daughter at her high school graduation. She squeezed my hand and said, "You've done your part, Dad." I smiled, but her words landed deep.

It was a moment of release, the culmination of years of small acts that had added up to something permanent.

I had poured myself out, and what remained was not exhaustion but peace.

That's the strange arithmetic of love: what you give away is never lost; it returns, transformed, in the lives you've shaped.

Leadership as Legacy

Leadership, too, finds its true measure not in what outlasts your tenure but in *who* does.

The finest leaders build successors, not monuments. They leave systems that function without them and people who flourish beyond them.

I once knew a CEO who said his proudest moment wasn't hitting a revenue target or winning an award, it was when one of his former interns became his peer. "That," he said, "was the day I knew I'd really led."

Leadership that hoards power dies with the leader.
Leadership that shares power lives on indefinitely.

To live a life poured out, you must make peace with anonymity, to bless people who may never know your name, to invest in work that might never carry your signature.

The legacy of service isn't about being remembered; it's about ensuring that goodness is.

The Rhythm of Renewal

To sustain a life of service, you must embrace a rhythm, giving and resting, pouring and being poured into.

I've learned that even the most selfless hearts need sabbath. Time to breathe. Time to listen again to the quiet voice that reminds you *why* you serve.

Without that rhythm, generosity becomes exhaustion disguised as virtue.

But when you live in balance, when you give deeply and rest honestly, service becomes art. You move through life like a well-played instrument, every note an act of alignment.

That rhythm produces joy, the joy of contribution without competition, of meaning without recognition.

That joy is what turns service from duty into delight.

The Abundance of Emptiness

As strange as it sounds, the people who give most often seem the most full, full of peace, of laughter, of perspective. It's as if generosity stretches the soul, making it capable of holding more life.

When I look at the lives of the truly great, those who loved deeply, led humbly, and served relentlessly, I see a common thread: they were all *light*. Not just morally luminous, but weightless.

Their identities weren't anchored to possessions or titles, but to contribution.

They understood something most of us only glimpse: that the purpose of a vessel is not to stay full, but to pour.

Self-Reflection

1. In what areas of your life are you still clinging when you could be contributing?

2. Who has been quietly pouring into you, and how might you honor or emulate them?

3. What would "enough" look like for you if service became your measure of success?

Habits that Matter

- **Pouring Inventory:** Write down where your time, energy, and attention flow each week. Are they aligned with what matters most?

- **Refill Practice:** Schedule one period of rest each week that is truly restorative, no screens, no striving. Let it renew your capacity to give.

- **Legacy Note:** Write a letter (to be given now or later) to someone who has shaped you through their service. Tell them what their giving has taught you.

- **Silent Blessing:** Perform one act of generosity this week for someone who will never know it was you.

Closing thought

A life poured out is not about grandeur; it's about grace. It's not about being empty; it's about being *available*.

Service expands the FatherFrame™ by shifting leadership from self-focus to others-focus, turning authority into influence.

And one day, when your influence has outlasted your role and your name has faded from the roster, the work of your hands and heart will remain, in the laughter you sparked, the courage you ignited, the kindness you multiplied.

That is the paradox of a life poured out:
What you release becomes what remains

Service shifts leadership from ego to purpose, but purpose finds its fullest expression in love. At some point in every leader's journey, the question emerges: *What drives me?* Service answers *how* we lead; love answers *why*.

Love is not the soft end of leadership, it is the sustaining fire that keeps all the other pillars alive. In the final chapter, we explore love as culture, courage, discipline, and decision. This is where the FatherFrame™ comes full circle, revealing the heart at the center of every meaningful act of leadership.

Chapter Eight — Leadership Is Love

"Love, expressed as courage, empathy, discipline, and care, is the ultimate leadership posture, turning authority into influence and teams into communities."

Love is leadership's most misunderstood and underrated force, not romantic or sentimental, but courageous, accountable, and deeply principled.

This chapter reveals that love is what binds all other leadership qualities together: presence, compassion, discipline, integrity, and service. When leaders operate from love, expressed as justice, empathy, truth, and care, workplaces become communities and teams become families.

Love is what strengthens culture, enables vulnerability, fuels resilience, and creates leaders people actually want to follow. It is not an emotion; it's a decision to lead with humanity.

Love is the integrating pillar of the FatherFrame™, the principle that binds presence, clarity, communication, compassion, and integrity into a leadership posture that is both courageous and deeply human. Love isn't softness; it is responsible, principled, and transformative. This chapter explores love as the highest expression of leadership.

At the Centre of All Things

If you strip leadership down to its truest core, what remains isn't strategy, charisma, or even vision.

It's love.

Love, not the romantic kind, nor the sentimental kind, but the fierce, steady, sacrificial kind, is the energy that makes presence possible, gives priorities meaning, sustains discipline, softens integrity, and breathes humanity into service.

Love is what keeps leaders awake when others sleep, not out of anxiety, but out of care.
It's what keeps parents showing up when exhaustion whispers, *Enough*.
It's what compels the weary to keep standing when cynicism feels easier.

Every other leadership virtue, honesty, courage, empathy, self-control, draws its life from love.

Because love, at its essence, is the decision to will the good of another, even when it costs you something.

The First Lessons of Love

I didn't learn love in the boardroom.
I learned it at home, in the slow, ordinary rhythm of family life.

Love is the small, unrecorded work that builds a life. It's in the early mornings making breakfast before the day begins. It's in the late-night conversation when someone's heart is heavy. It's in the unspoken sacrifices that no one will ever see.

Parenthood teaches you that love isn't measured in moments of emotion but in *accumulated constancy*.

The same is true in leadership.
Love isn't expressed in speeches; it's proven in consistency.

It's staying calm in crisis.
It's telling the truth when lying would be easier.
It's forgiving when resentment would feel justified.

Love is the invisible infrastructure that keeps every organization, and every family, standing.

The Leadership of Care
Leadership divorced from love becomes manipulation.
It's power without compassion, vision without humanity.

But leadership infused with love becomes stewardship, the careful tending of souls, not just systems.

I've sat in rooms where leaders talked endlessly about metrics and performance, but not once about people. You could feel the vacuum, the slow erosion of meaning.

Then I've walked into teams led by love, where kindness isn't policy but instinct, where people look out for each other, where laughter and truth coexist. Those places hum with quiet excellence.

Love, in the practical sense, is what makes accountability safe, ambition healthy, and excellence sustainable.

Love doesn't weaken performance; it *grounds* it. It creates psychological safety, emotional loyalty, and moral courage, the kind of culture where people give their best not because they must, but because they *want* to.

The Fusion of Strength and Softness
Love is both steel and silk.

It's not passive acceptance, nor indulgent tolerance. It's strength wrapped in gentleness, the kind of strength that protects without overpowering, the kind of gentleness that speaks truth without wounding.

When love governs leadership, confrontation becomes restoration, not condemnation. Feedback becomes care. Discipline becomes investment.

In a family, love sets boundaries not to restrict, but to nurture. In an organization, love sets standards not to punish, but to refine.

The aim is the same in both: growth rooted in safety, accountability anchored in affection.

Love, when mature, doesn't flinch from truth. It just tells it kindly.

The Heart that Holds Many

To lead is to hold many hearts, to absorb disappointment without retaliation, to celebrate others' success without envy, to keep loving when the love is not returned.

That's the hardest part of leadership: loving people who may never fully understand the cost of your love.

But that's what fathers do. That's what good leaders do. They keep giving, not because it's reciprocated, but because love has become their nature.

And in that, there is quiet freedom.

Love doesn't wait for worthiness; it creates it.

Self-Reflection

1. What does "leadership as love" mean to you in practice, not theory?

2. Who, in your sphere, most needs a leader's love right now, patience, presence, belief?

3. How might you lead with affection without losing accountability?

Habits that Matter

- **Love Audit:** Reflect on your week and note where love was missing from your leadership decisions. Where could care replace criticism?

- **Affirmation Habit:** Once a day, name someone's effort out loud, not their result, their *heart*.

- **Reconnection:** Identify one relationship where your leadership has grown distant. Reach out, not to fix, but to reconnect.

- **Pause of Presence:** Before entering any meeting or family moment, take one breath and silently remind yourself: *Lead with love.*

Love as Discipline and Decision

Love, at its most enduring, isn't a feeling that swells and fades with circumstance. It's a decision repeated daily, an act of disciplined will.

It doesn't depend on mood or convenience. It's not limited to warmth or affection. Love, in its mature form, is a *choice to act for the good of another*, even when fatigue whispers "not today," even when pride demands repayment, even when fear urges retreat.

This kind of love, the love that leads, is forged in repetition, like any skill. It's muscle memory of the soul.

The Quiet Courage of Choosing Love

The hardest part of love isn't beginning, it's continuing.

Anyone can be kind when emotions are aligned, when gratitude is returned, when effort is noticed. But love is most powerful when it persists without recognition.

In leadership, this looks like extending grace after being misunderstood. It's choosing patience over punishment when frustration burns hot. It's offering another chance when results have disappointed.

At home, it's the parent who keeps showing up to talk, even after the slammed door. The partner who forgives not because the pain was small, but because the relationship is larger.

That's love as discipline, the daily choice to keep heart open when it would be easier to close it.

It's not the absence of boundaries; it's the refusal to let bitterness build them.

Love says, *I will not let your weakness shrink my capacity to care.*

Love and the Leader's Will

Discipline and will are often described in cold terms, grit, determination, toughness. But love redefines them.

The strongest leaders are not those who impose their will, but those who *train it*.

They learn to master emotion without suppressing empathy, to act consistently when impulse would dictate otherwise.

When love shapes the will, leadership becomes less about control and more about conviction.

I once worked with a director who led a large team through a messy transition. Every week brought new setbacks, angry calls, lost contracts, sleepless nights. One afternoon I found her in the hallway, leaning against the wall, eyes closed. "You okay?" I asked.

She nodded, exhaling slowly. "I just keep reminding myself, love doesn't quit on people."

It wasn't naïveté. It was stamina born of compassion, the kind of inner training that keeps a leader kind under pressure.

Love, disciplined, becomes endurance.

The Fatigue of Care

There's a unique exhaustion that comes with caring deeply.

When you lead or parent with love, you open yourself to disappointment, to misunderstanding, to heartbreak. And sometimes the cost feels too high.

That's when love's discipline becomes essential, because the will must take over where emotion ends.

You learn to rest, not to resign.
You learn to pause, not to withdraw.
You learn that love, like any practice, requires recovery.

Even compassion needs boundaries to stay healthy. Without them, love becomes martyrdom instead of leadership.

The discipline of love is not about giving endlessly, it's about giving *wisely*. It's saying yes to what builds and no to what drains.

Sometimes the most loving act is saying "enough," because love without self-respect eventually erodes both parties.

True love disciplines itself to remain sustainable.

Love and Accountability
Love is not indulgent. It doesn't coddle or condone.

Real love holds people accountable, not out of anger, but out of respect.

A father disciplines not to dominate, but to guide. A leader shouldn't correct to humiliate, but to restore integrity.

The tone of love changes everything. Accountability delivered through frustration feels like punishment; accountability delivered through love feels like belief.

I once watched a manager sit with an underperforming staff member. Instead of beginning with criticism, she began with conviction: "I believe you're capable of better than this. Let's figure out why you're stuck."

That sentence reframed the entire conversation. The employee left encouraged, not shamed, motivated to improve rather than defend.

That's the difference between love as emotion and love as discipline: one demands apology, the other invites transformation.

The Discipline of Staying
Perhaps the hardest discipline of all is simply staying, staying when trust is fragile, staying when the outcome is uncertain, staying when affection feels one-sided.

Love doesn't always look like tenderness; sometimes it looks like perseverance.

In leadership, staying might mean walking with a struggling team through restructuring instead of escaping to a cleaner opportunity. In family, it might mean showing up for a child who's pushing you away, or for a partner weathering their own internal storm.

The staying heart is the strongest kind. It doesn't stay out of obligation but out of commitment to what could still be redeemed.

Because love, in its disciplined form, is faith in motion, the belief that something good can still grow here.

Love's Small Disciplines
Big gestures of love are rare. But small, disciplined acts of love are constant, and they are the scaffolding of every enduring relationship and every healthy organization.

It's the follow-up message after a hard conversation.
It's the handwritten note when words feel inadequate.
It's the choice to pause before reacting, to listen before advising, to understand before correcting.

These habits, practised daily, build invisible strength.

Over time, they form a pattern, not of perfection, but of persistence.

The people under your care, your children, your colleagues, your friends, come to trust that your love is not mood-dependent. They can rest in it.

That's how love earns its authority, through repetition, not rhetoric.

Self-Reflection

1. Where in your life has love become a feeling instead of a disciplined choice?

2. What relationship or responsibility is calling for the endurance of love, not the ease of withdrawal?

3. How can accountability in your world become an act of love rather than control?

Habits that Matter

- **Love Rehearsal:** Choose one relationship where frustration has replaced patience. For one week, practice one small, consistent act of care, without expecting reciprocation.

- **Pause Practice:** When tempted to react sharply, pause long enough to ask, "What would love do here?" Then do that.

- **Accountability with Affection:** In your next difficult feedback conversation, lead with belief in the person's potential. Let correction come from confidence, not criticism.

- **Renewal Routine:** Build one act of rest into your leadership rhythm each week, something that refills your capacity to love.

The Vulnerability of Leadership

There is a certain armor we all learn to wear when we step into leadership. It's woven from confidence, competence, and control, the traits that make others feel safe in our hands. But the longer we wear that armor, the heavier it becomes.

Eventually, it begins to separate us from the very people we are trying to serve.

Love, real love, asks something far more courageous than command, it asks for *exposure*.

To lead with love is to lead with an undefended heart. It's to risk being misunderstood, to stand open-handed in a world that rewards self-protection. It's to admit that you don't have all the answers, and to trust that people will still follow you, not because you're flawless, but because you're *true*.

As Brené Brown reminds us, vulnerability isn't weakness, it's the birthplace of courage and connection. Love, in leadership, begins with the willingness to be seen as imperfect and still worthy of trust.

The Courage to Be Seen

In a culture obsessed with image, vulnerability feels like heresy. We are told to polish, to perform, to present the highlight reel.

But people don't connect with perfection. They connect with honesty.

I once worked with a senior leader whose team was collapsing under pressure. Morale was low, targets were missed, and the atmosphere had turned brittle. After weeks of silence, he called an all-hands meeting. We expected another tactical briefing. Instead, he began with this:

"I haven't been myself lately. I've been scared, scared of failing you, scared of losing control. And I think that fear's been leaking into how I lead."

The room went silent, not out of judgment, but out of relief. For the first time, people exhaled. Someone finally spoke the truth everyone could feel.

That moment turned everything. Productivity didn't spike overnight, but trust did. And from trust came momentum.

Vulnerability didn't weaken his authority; it deepened it. Because love, when expressed through humility, makes strength accessible.

The Father's Mirror
Parenthood teaches vulnerability in its purest form.

When you love a child, you are perpetually exposed. Their pain becomes your own. Their mistakes feel personal. Their silence can wound deeper than words.

You quickly learn that you cannot lead them through control, only through connection.

There was a night my teenage daughter came home late, her tone sharp, her walls high. The father in me wanted to lecture. The leader in me wanted to correct. But something softer in me, something *wiser*, told me to pause.

Instead, I said quietly, "You seem angry. I probably deserve some of that. Tell me what's really going on."

The conversation that followed was messy, emotional, honest. But it was real.

And that reality strengthened us more than any discipline ever could have.

That's the strange grace of vulnerability: when you stop protecting yourself, you make it safe for others to come out of hiding too.

The Myth of Invincibility

The modern myth of leadership is invincibility, the belief that strength is measured by what we can endure without breaking.

But invulnerability isn't strength; it's separation. It isolates the leader and suffocates empathy.

Teams and families don't need untouchable heroes. They need human beings who model recovery, not just resilience.

The Professor and researcher, Brené Brown calls this *wholehearted leadership*, the willingness to show up when you can't control the outcome.

I've watched leaders apologize to their teams, cry in front of their children, or confess when they didn't know what to do. Far from diminishing them, those moments made them magnetic. People rallied to their honesty.

Because when you lead without armor, others lower theirs too. Authenticity is contagious.

The Fear of Exposure

Vulnerability feels dangerous because it is. It opens the door to misunderstanding, disappointment, even betrayal.

But the alternative, a life sealed off by pride, is far more dangerous.

A leader who cannot be vulnerable cannot be known.
A father who cannot be vulnerable cannot be trusted.

And people cannot follow what they cannot trust.

It's natural to fear exposure. But love gives you the courage to accept that risk, because connection is worth it.

There's a tenderness in every act of vulnerability, a quiet defiance against cynicism. Each time you tell the truth about your weakness, you reclaim a piece of your humanity. Each time you choose empathy over image, you invite others to do the same.

The result is not chaos, but communion, a team or family that breathes together, anchored in truth.

The Practice of Transparency
Vulnerability in leadership doesn't mean oversharing; it means *accurate sharing.* It's the skill of revealing enough to create connection, not confusion.

It's saying, "I'm uncertain about this direction, but I believe in our capacity to figure it out."
Or, "I made a mistake, and I'm learning from it."
Or even, "That decision hurt me too."

These statements signal safety. They tell people: *We are human here.*

I once led through a round of difficult restructures, the kind that shake trust at every level. I decided to hold an open forum, no slides, no script.

Someone asked bluntly, "Do you even care about what this is doing to us?"

I took a breath and said, "Yes. Absolutely. I hate it. But I believe it's necessary. And I'm here to walk through the hard parts with you and be accountable."

Silence again, the kind that feels like collective reflection. Then someone nodded. Another person spoke up. And slowly, the conversation turned from accusation to participation.

That day I learned that people can handle almost any truth, as long as they know they're not facing it alone.

That's what love does. It doesn't erase pain; it stands inside it.

The Leader as Listener

Vulnerability is not only about speaking truth; it's about creating space for others to do the same.

The servant-leader listens without agenda, hears without defense, and allows others' emotions to exist without trying to fix them.

Listening deeply is one of the most vulnerable acts in leadership because it demands stillness, the surrender of control, the willingness to be affected by what you hear.

In that stillness, love listens not just to respond, but to *understand*. And understanding, once it takes root, becomes wisdom.

Strength Through Softness

When we think of leadership and love, we often picture contrasts: strong versus soft, decisive versus tender. But the highest form of strength is the ability to be both.

It takes power to stand open when you could stand guarded. It takes courage to admit fault in front of those who depend on you. It takes moral clarity to stay gentle in a world that rewards aggression.

Love doesn't weaken leadership; it completes it.

Because love doesn't strip power away, it refines it, filters it through empathy, and makes it safe.

Self-Reflection

1. Where are you hiding behind competence instead of honesty?

2. What truth could free your team or your family if you were brave enough to speak it?

3. How might your vulnerability become someone else's permission to heal?

Habits that Matter

- **Truth Share:** Identify one area where you've been holding back for fear of appearing weak. Share that truth with someone you lead or love.

- **Open Forum:** In your next meeting or family discussion, invite others to express what they need from you, without defense. Just listen.

- **Emotional Check-In:** Once a week, ask yourself: "What am I really feeling beneath the work?" Write it down, name it before it hardens.

- **Forgive Yourself:** Choose one mistake you're still carrying. Speak forgiveness aloud, not as excuse, but as release.

Love as Culture

Every organization, like every family, eventually reveals what it loves most. You can see it in what gets rewarded, what gets tolerated, and what people whisper when no one's watching. Love, in that sense, is not a feeling, it's a culture. It's what remains when the policies fade and the personalities move on.

There's a well known description of love that I've always found quietly timeless, not because of its poetry, but because of its practicality.

Love is patient, love is kind. It does not envy, it does not boast, it is not proud. It does not dishonour others, it is not self-seeking, it is not easily angered, it keeps no record of wrongs. Love does not delight in evil but rejoices with the truth. It always protects, always trusts, always hopes, always perseveres.

I've heard those words at weddings, but I've seen their truth in boardrooms. Because that description of love isn't sentimental, it's structural. It's a blueprint for how people can lead and live together when power, ego, and pressure are all in play.

Love is patient, the leader who takes time to understand before judging, who gives people room to grow rather than rushing them to perform.

Love is kind, the leader who corrects without crushing, who treats honesty as a form of kindness, not cruelty.

It does not envy or boast, the leader who celebrates others' success without insecurity, who finds joy in another's win.

It is not proud, the leader who says, "I was wrong," before they're forced to.

It does not dishonour others, the leader who speaks of those absent with the same respect they show in person.

It keeps no record of wrongs, the leader who sees mistakes as part of growth, not ammunition for later.

And finally, it always protects, always trusts, always hopes, always perseveres, the leader who guards the culture like something sacred, who assumes the best even when performance dips, who keeps believing in people until they rediscover belief in themselves.

These lines, when lived rather than quoted, become the architecture of a healthy organization. They describe a love that doesn't live in words or sentiment, but in *decisions*: to protect rather than punish, to trust rather than control, to hope rather than harden.

In that way, love becomes culture, not as emotion, but as alignment. It's how patience becomes process, how kindness becomes policy, how trust becomes habit.

When teams experience this kind of love, they don't just comply; they *belong*. Performance becomes purpose with a heartbeat. Accountability feels like safety, not surveillance.

Because love, real love, is not the soft side of leadership. It's the strong side. It's the discipline that endures when charisma fades, the decision that keeps showing up long after motivation runs out.

In the end, love as culture is what every great leader builds, whether they use that word or not. It's what makes homes safe, workplaces humane, and legacies worth inheriting.

Love, when sustained long enough, begins to move beyond the heart of an individual.

It becomes atmosphere.
It becomes architecture.
It becomes *culture*.

Homes, teams, and organizations that operate on love don't always use that word. They may talk about "trust," "values," "respect," or "wellbeing." But beneath every healthy culture, if you dig deep enough, you'll find the same root system, people who have chosen to care, consistently.

Love, in the context of leadership, is not sentiment. It's *structure*.

It's the set of shared assumptions that define how we treat one another when things go wrong, how we celebrate when things go right, and how we show up in between.

Robert Sternberg's Triangular Theory of Love describes love as a combination of intimacy, passion, and commitment. In leadership, these translate to connection, conviction, and constancy, the three dimensions of trust.

The Atmosphere of Grace
Every culture has a climate, a prevailing emotional temperature.

In some workplaces, it's tense and cold; in others, warm and trusting.

In families, the air can be thick with fear or light with forgiveness.

What determines that temperature is not mission statements or slogans, it's the leader's emotional tone.

A leader who leads with love changes the weather.

Love creates grace, not the absence of standards, but the presence of understanding.

It's what allows mistakes to become lessons instead of liabilities. It's what turns feedback into growth rather than shame.

In one organization I advised, a manager began every weekly meeting by asking a simple question: *"Who needs a little grace this week?"*

It was half joke, half ritual, but it changed everything. People began to share honestly about exhaustion, about missed deadlines, about the emotional weight of care work.

The result wasn't lowered performance. It was *increased trust*.

Grace, it turns out, is the soil where excellence grows best.

From Policy to Practice
Love can't be legislated into a culture. You can't write a policy that says, "Be kind."

You can, however, create systems that make kindness easier and cruelty harder.

Culture shifts not through speeches but through *structure*.

When leaders build rhythms that prioritize empathy, listening sessions, flexible boundaries, recognition rituals, they transform love from an aspiration into an operating system.

I've seen this in volunteer organizations, where gratitude is built into every meeting. Before tackling business, the chairperson asks each person to name one thing they appreciated about someone else that week.

It takes ten minutes, but the payoff is profound: people begin to see each other not as cogs but as contributors. It turns transactions into relationships.

In families, similar rituals form culture too, the shared meal, the bedtime talk, the check-in on hard days. These small habits encode love into memory.

Love becomes not a feeling, but a *practice you participate in daily*.

The Economics of Care
Cultures run on what they value.

If profit is the only currency, people will trade integrity for results.

If control is the currency, they'll trade creativity for safety.

One organization I had come to know, had a mission statement that included the words "Increase shareholder value". It always made me ask – at what cost?

But when care becomes the currency, everything changes.

People stop competing for approval and start collaborating for purpose.

Innovation rises because fear falls.

Performance becomes sustainable because burnout declines.

One executive I knew measured success in what she called "care velocity", the speed at which compassion moved through her organization. She paid attention not just to performance metrics but to *response times of kindness*: how long it took for someone to be noticed when struggling, thanked when succeeding, or supported when uncertain.

It was unconventional. It was also incredibly effective. Turnover dropped. Trust rose. Teams performed better.

Because in every measurable way, love proved to be good business.

In homes, this same principle applies. Care economies thrive when generosity outpaces grievance, when you forgive faster than you criticize, and thank quicker than you demand.

Love, when practiced communally, creates a compound return.

Love as Shared Language
Cultures shaped by love develop their own dialects, words, gestures, and rituals that reinforce belonging.

In one retail organization I visited, staff used the phrase *"Caught you caring"* as part of their internal recognition. Any employee could nominate another for small acts of kindness, covering a shift, mentoring a new hire, offering encouragement.

Each week, a few stories were read aloud at their team huddle. They called it "Love in Action," though they never used the word "love" in corporate documents. It was simply the DNA of who they were.

In families, the same phenomenon occurs. A shared phrase like "I'm proud of you," or a simple nightly "Goodnight, I love you", repeated thousands of times over years, becomes the soundtrack of security.

Words form worlds.

When love governs language, it shapes how people interpret failure, success, and each other.

Love teaches people to see through the lens of *we* rather than *me*.

The Hard Edges of Love
It's easy to think of love-filled cultures as soft or conflict-averse. But love has edges, and sharp ones.

A culture built on love does not avoid confrontation; it redeems it.

It allows disagreement without disrespect, correction without contempt.

In one faith-based organization I was a part of, they had a rule of engagement called "grace and truth." Every tough conversation was expected to hold both. If you were confronting a behavior, you began with affirmation. If you were delivering praise, you also offered perspective.

It wasn't about politeness; it was about alignment, ensuring that love stayed real, not sentimental.

True love cultures are not free of tension. They're just free of *fear*.

And that difference makes all the difference.

Scaling Love
People often ask whether love can really scale, whether empathy and compassion can survive in large systems.

The answer is yes, but only if it's modelled.

Culture is simply leadership multiplied.
When love begins in the heart of one leader and is practiced with consistency, it replicates.

Each act of patience sets precedent. Each story of kindness becomes folklore. Each apology made by someone in power becomes permission for everyone else to be human too.

That's how love scales: not by declaration, but by demonstration.

Self-Reflection

1. What is the "emotional temperature" of the culture you lead — and how does your tone influence it?

2. What habits or rituals could encode love more tangibly into your family, team, or organization?

3. Where could grace, not guilt, become the engine of accountability?

Habits that Matter

- **Cultural Audit:** Observe your environment for one week. What gets celebrated? What gets punished? What does that reveal about your true values?

- **Grace Habit:** Begin your next team or family meeting by naming one person who demonstrated kindness. Make that rhythm normal.

- **Language Shift:** Replace one transactional phrase (e.g., "output," "performance") with one relational phrase (e.g., "growth," "care") in your daily speech.

- **Temperature Check:** Once a month, ask people, "How safe do you feel to speak truth here?" Track the answers like you would a financial report.

The Lasting Fire

There comes a moment in every life of leadership when ambition burns itself out, when the trophies gather dust, when the calendar quiets and the accolades stop echoing. And in that silence, what remains is the only thing that was ever real, *love*.

Love is the lasting fire.

It's the warmth that endures when strategy fades, the light that keeps burning long after you've stepped away from the desk, the home, or the stage.

It is what those who knew you will feel, not what they will say about you, but what they will *carry from you*.

The Fire That Outlives the Flame

The paradox of fire is that it must consume itself to give light. It diminishes physically even as it radiates more powerfully.

So it is with love.

Every time you pour yourself into others, mentoring, teaching, comforting, guiding, you give something away. But instead of emptiness, you create illumination. You set small fires in other hearts, and those fires spread in directions you'll never see.

Love's economy is not measured in what's kept but in what's kindled.

The father who teaches patience to his child lights a flame that may warm generations.

The leader who gives grace instead of anger teaches others that kindness is not weakness but wisdom.

The friend who forgives models what courage really looks like.

You cannot trace the full trajectory of love. You can only trust that its warmth outlives you.

Love as Leadership's Afterglow

Every leader eventually leaves. Every parent eventually steps back. Every role, no matter how influential, has an end date.

But love leaves residue, a kind of invisible legacy that lingers in tone, in culture, in memory.

People might forget your words, your plans, even your name, but they will remember how you made them feel.

That is love's afterglow.

When a workplace feels lighter because you once led there. When a home feels safer because of how you once listened. When someone somewhere makes a kinder choice because of the way you once treated them.

That's the true succession plan, not titles, not systems, but transformed hearts.

Leadership built on ego ends when you leave the room. Leadership built on love continues long after.

The Refining Fire

Fire purifies what it touches. So does love.

It burns away the dross, the pretense, the pride, the fear, until what remains is gold: humility, clarity, truth.

In leadership, love refines our motives. It asks us: *Why are you doing this?*
To be admired, or to make others whole?
To build something impressive, or to build something enduring?

Love as fire doesn't coddle; it cleanses. It forces honesty about where our energy is going and what truly matters.

Many leaders discover, too late, that their brilliance came at the expense of their relationships. The smarter ones learn early to let love burn away their illusions, that achievement equals worth, or that control equals safety.

What remains after love's refining flame is the one thing that can't be destroyed by success or failure: purpose.

Love doesn't just drive great work; it *purifies* the reasons we work at all.

The Tenderness of Legacy
We often think of legacy in monumental terms, endowments, institutions, innovations. But love's legacy is far quieter.

It lives in tone, not texture.
In memory, not material.
In the unseen gestures that ripple through time.

I once attended the funeral of a community leader, not a famous man, but one who had served faithfully for decades. People came from everywhere. There were no CEOs, no headlines. Just stories.

A young woman stood and said, "He remembered my name when no one else did."

Another said, "He believed in me before I believed in myself."

There were hundreds of stories like that. Tiny moments. Invisible on paper. Eternal in effect.

And I thought: *This is the kind of success worth living for.*

Love is the only thing that survives translation across generations. Everything else, wealth, power, reputation, loses its meaning outside its time. But love translates fluently into every language, every century.

That is why it is the last fire worth tending

The Fire That Renews
The great secret of love is that it doesn't just endure, it renews.

When you live and lead with love, you stop chasing relevance and start cultivating radiance. You no longer fear the fading of youth, the slowing of seasons, the shifting of roles. Because the source of your worth is not external.

Love has no retirement. It changes shape but not strength.

In youth, love acts. In maturity, love steadies. In age, love blesses.

The hands that once built now hold. The voice that once commanded now comforts. The leader who once drove results now multiplies wisdom through gentleness.

And that, perhaps, is the highest evolution of leadership, to become a presence that no longer needs to prove anything, only to give.

Love's fire burns cleanest when it no longer needs to consume.

A Father's Benediction
As I write these final reflections, I think of my own children, of the hope that one day they'll lead with love, not because they read it in a book, but because they *felt* it at home.

If there's any truth, I'd want them to inherit, it's this:
Leadership is not about being in charge. It's about being in *care*.

If you can hold that truth, if you can love with both courage and humility, you'll never truly run out of light.

Because in the end, leadership is simply love in motion, the ongoing act of turning care into influence, compassion into change, presence into peace.

And when your own flame begins to dim, the fires you've kindled in others will keep the world warm.

That's what makes love the lasting fire.

Self-Reflection

1. What remains when everything you've built is gone?

2. Whose warmth in your life still glows from a fire lit long ago?

3. What would it look like to lead in such a way that your absence still radiates light?

Habits that Matter

- **Legacy Journal:** Write down three moments this month where you led with love instead of fear. Track how those moments shifted outcomes.

- **Blessing Habit:** End each week by quietly blessing someone in your world, through encouragement, prayer, or silent gratitude.

- **Simplify and Tend:** Choose one relationship or project that matters most and invest love into it, not efficiency, not control, but love.

- **Carry the Fire:** Before sleep, ask yourself: *Did I warm anyone today?*

Closing thought

The leader's heart and the father's heart are one and the same. Both exist to give life, to cultivate hope, to leave light.

May your leadership burn bright, not for applause, but for warmth.

Love completes the FatherFrame™, the integrating force that binds every principle together and shapes leaders who elevate the lives of others.

Because in the end, the truest measure of life is not how long it burns, but how far its fire travels.

Love completes the circle, but it also pulls the circle wider. When you've seen how presence steadies, priorities clarify, communication connects, discipline strengthens, compassion softens, integrity aligns, and service expands, love gathers them all into one coherent, generous way of being. Before we close, the FatherFrame™ synthesis draws these threads together, showing how these eight pillars do not stand alone but interdependently. This final integration invites you to see the whole model as one living, breathing posture of leadership.

The FatherFramed™ Leader — A Closing Synthesis

Across these pages, eight principles have resurfaced again and again, not as abstract theory, but as lived moments drawn from family life, leadership challenges, hard-earned lessons, and quiet observations. You've seen them in the stories at the breakfast table, in boardrooms under pressure, in mistakes made, and in moments redeemed. Each principle stands on its own, yet none of them work in isolation. Together, they form the FatherFrame™, a way of leading that is calm, clear, compassionate, and unmistakably human.

Presence steadies the people we lead.
Priorities give shape to what matters most.
Communication builds bridges of trust and truth.
Discipline creates the reliability that others rely on.
Compassion restores dignity and strengthens relationships.
Integrity anchors leadership in character, not convenience.
Service turns influence outward, lifting the people around us.
Love binds all of it together with courage, humility, and purpose.

These are not corporate competencies or parental techniques.

They are postures of the heart, ways of being that shape the atmosphere around us. They form a rhythm of leadership that works in every setting, because it begins with something universal: the desire to help others grow.

Leadership is not merely the act of directing; it is the daily decision to show up with presence, to choose wisely, to speak truthfully, to act consistently, to understand deeply, to stand firmly, to give generously, and to love courageously. This is what transforms leadership from performance into relationship, from authority into influence, and from pressure into purpose.

The FatherFrame™ is not a model to memorize but a mirror to return to, a reminder of the leader you are becoming and the legacy you are shaping with every conversation, every decision, every act of attention.

In the end, the question is not "How well did I lead?"
The question is, "Who became better because I was their leader?"

If even one person breathes easier, grows stronger, or sees themselves differently because of your presence, then you are already leading like a father, regardless of whether you have children of your own.

This is the work.
This is the legacy.
This is FatherFramed™ Leadership.

Epilogue

By the time you reach this final page, you may notice something subtle: every chapter has really been about love. Presence is love paying attention. Priorities are love choosing wisely. Emotional intelligence is love that listens. Values are love made consistent. Legacy is love that outlives you. These truths don't just belong to families; they belong to leadership.

Because leadership rarely announces itself. It reveals itself in the quiet moments: when someone turns to you for reassurance, when your words lift a weight, when your presence steadies a room that feels unravelling. These moments never appear in strategy papers or performance dashboards, yet they are the moments people remember. They are the moments that shape stories.

The FatherFrame™ simply gives language to what you already know in your bones: the qualities that help children grow also help teams flourish, and the principles that make families strong also make organizations healthy. Leadership is not something we switch on at work and off at home, it is who we are becoming, everywhere.

And this work is not about perfection. You will not embody presence every day. You will not always choose courage over comfort or empathy over judgement. Neither will I. Leadership is not a performance to master; it is a practice to return to, again and again, with humility and hope. What matters is not flawless consistency but the quiet, repeated choices that form the atmosphere people feel around you.

That atmosphere is your leadership.

As Maya Angelou reminds us, people may forget what you taught them, but they will never forget how you made them feel. The same is true of those we lead. They remember whether they felt understood, supported, safe, and strengthened by your presence. Leadership is emotional work, and emotional work is human work.

The leaders who shaped my life all shared one thing: they saw people, not problems. They led with hearts engaged and egos at rest. They created belonging. They left others better than they found them.

As you close this book, I hope you open a new chapter in your own leadership, one where wisdom and warmth walk hand in hand. Not because you've adopted a new model, but because you've recognized the leader you already are, and the leader you are still becoming. Someone in your world, at work, at home, or in your community, will look to you for steadiness. When that moment comes, I hope you feel its weight and its wonder and choose to lead with love.

Because the world has enough bosses.
What it needs are leaders who choose presence over pressure, compassion over certainty, and belonging over bureaucracy.
Leaders who love people into growth.
Leaders who lead like fathers.

References

Bass, B. M., & Avolio, B. J. (1994). Improving Organizational Effectiveness Through Transformational Leadership.

Brown, B. (2012). Daring Greatly: How the Courage to Be Vulnerable Transforms the Way We Live, Love, Parent, and Lead.

Cathy, D. T. (2014). It's Easier to Succeed Than to Fail.

Covey, S. R. (1989). The 7 Habits of Highly Effective People.

Edmondson, A. (2019). The Fearless Organization: Creating Psychological Safety in the Workplace for Learning, Innovation, and Growth.

Fredrickson, B. (2009). Positivity.

Goleman, D. (1995). Emotional Intelligence: Why It Can Matter More Than IQ.

Greenleaf, R. K. (1977). Servant Leadership: A Journey into the Nature of Legitimate Power and Greatness.

McKeown, G. (2014). Essentialism: The Disciplined Pursuit of Less.

Polman, P. (2021). Net Positive: How Courageous Companies Thrive by Giving More Than They Take.

Schultz, H. (2011). Onward: How Starbucks Fought for Its Life Without Losing Its Soul.

Senge, P. (1990). The Fifth Discipline: The Art & Practice of The Learning Organization.

Stanley, A. (2006). Visioneering: God's Blueprint for Developing and Maintaining Vision.

Acknowledgements:

To every father, mentor, and leader who taught me that leadership is first a responsibility of the heart, thank you.

To my family, who teach me daily how to lead with patience, consistency and humor.

And to the teams I've been privileged to serve, you have been my greatest classroom.

About the Author

Mark Jeffery is a Leadership practitioner and executive known for his work in applying positive psychology and emotional intelligence to real-world organizational change. With over twenty-five years of leadership, Mark brings a deeply human approach to transformation, anchored in empathy, presence, and purpose.

A qualified Human Resource professional, Social and Emotional Intelligence Coach, and a graduate in Organizational Wellbeing, Mark has spent his career leading people through complexity with heart and strategy in equal measure. Mark has built a reputation for creating cultures of trust and resilience.

Mark's leadership philosophy bridges home and workplace, showing that the same principles that build strong families also build strong organizations. His writing draws on insights from Daniel Goleman's emotional intelligence, Robert Greenleaf's servant leadership, and Amy Edmondson's psychological safety, blending research with reflective storytelling to help leaders act with clarity, courage, and care.

Mark is also the creator of the FatherFramed™ Leadership Model, an evidence-informed framework grounded in the everyday wisdom of fatherhood. The model translates the timeless strengths of great fathers into practical, human-centered leadership principles for modern workplaces.

A father first, Mark, writes from lived experience about the intersection of leadership and love. His central message is simple but transformative: leadership begins at home, and the best leaders lead like fathers, not bosses.

www.ingramcontent.com/pod-product-compliance
Lightning Source LLC
Chambersburg PA
CBHW071546210326
41597CB00019B/3139